Agile Rx: A Prescription to Guide Agile Leaders

Daniel Silverman

Published by Momentrek Solutions, LLC, 2024.

Table of Contents

To my wife for always telling me to just publish all my writings, here's one.

To my parents for making me possible.

To Hunter, Kim, Celia, Max, and Lucy.

" Agile Rx"

"Daniel Silverman"

Agile Rx

A Prescription For Agile Leaders

Daniel Silverman

one

Introduction

This book should serve as guidance to leaders and future leaders in the agile space trying to gain knowledge and perspective on how to be better in our roles.

I wrote this book after almost two decades of coaching, consulting, and being a part of many different agile transformations. This experience includes being "in the trenches" and being an Agile Leader.

I've been asked many times, "Have you ever thought about writing a book about Agile and your experiences?"

My answer has always been, "No, but I have thought about writing a book on 'How To Fail at Agile'. I've felt there were already many books that try to offer wisdom on how to do agile well. However, if there was a book that showed us how to fail at it and that put an emphasis on what it takes to NOT succeed with Agile, there would be more to learn from it.

In some ways, this book is a compromise. There's a balance of what you should be thinking about to do well, but there's also honest insight into what causes failure.

It's also written in a modular way where you may not even have to read the entire book to find value.

You might be able to read the next chapter and know everything you need to know about Agile.

Everything You Need To Know About Agile

Value.

Adapt.

Improve.

three

Challenge

I am serious about the previous chapter. Those three words are all you need to understand to be successful at Agile.

You need to constantly be aware of what the highest VALUE is and your teams should always focus on delivering it to your customers and users.

With the fast changes that come, both from internal and external motivations, the ability to ADAPT with little to no resistance or pain is crucial.

Finally, we need a relentless state of being to always strive to IMPROVE, every second of every day, with every component of our system and processes.

If you are doing those three things, you will be successful every time.

However, I am aware it is always more complicated than that. Primarily because not everyone involved is aware of the importance of those three things to make Agile work. I wouldn't have been able to write the remaining words in this book if that was so.

As agile leaders, we are tasked with the responsibility of guiding our teams towards success in an ever-changing landscape. However, this journey is not without its fair share of challenges.

In this book, we will explore the key obstacles faced by agile leaders today and how Agile Rx offers valuable insights to overcome them.

1. Navigating Uncertainty: One of the greatest challenges faced by agile leaders is navigating uncertainty. The fast-paced nature of today's business environment demands quick decision-making and adaptability.

However, it can be difficult to strike a balance between being decisive and remaining flexible.

Agile Rx provides understanding for embracing uncertainty through its core principles. By fostering a culture of continuous learning and experimentation, agile leaders can empower their teams to embrace change and make informed decisions in the face of uncertainty.

2. Managing Stakeholder Expectations: Another challenge that often plagues agile leaders is managing stakeholder expectations. With multiple stakeholders involved in any project, each with its own set of priorities and demands, it can be challenging to strike a balance that satisfies everyone. Agile Rx emphasizes effective communication as a means to manage stakeholder expectations successfully. By establishing clear channels of communication and involving stakeholders throughout the process, agile leaders can ensure alignment and foster collaboration.

3. Overcoming Resistance to Change: Change is never easy, especially when it disrupts established routines or processes within an organization. Agile leaders often encounter resistance from team members who are hesitant to embrace new ways of working.

Agile Rx recognizes the importance of addressing resistance head-on through open dialogue and active engagement with team members. By providing support, resources, and training opportunities, agile leaders can help their teams overcome resistance to change while emphasizing the benefits that agility brings.

4. Balancing Short-term Results with Long-term Vision: In an era driven by immediate results, striking a balance between short-term goals and long-term vision becomes a significant challenge for agile leaders. It can be tempting to focus solely on quick wins and lose sight of the bigger picture. Agile Rx encourages agile leaders to maintain a long-term perspective while also celebrating short-term successes.

By setting clear goals and regularly reviewing progress, leaders can ensure that their teams stay on track toward the larger vision.

5. Building and Sustaining High-Performing Teams: Building and sustaining high-performing teams is a challenge that every agile leader faces. It requires

finding the right balance of skills, fostering collaboration, and empowering individuals to take ownership of their work. Agile Rx provides insights into effective team-building strategies such as forming cross-functional teams, promoting psychological safety, and encouraging continuous feedback.

By implementing these strategies, agile leaders can create an environment where high performance becomes the norm.

Conclusion: As agile leaders, we are constantly faced with challenges that test our ability to adapt and lead in dynamic environments. Agile Rx offers valuable insights into overcoming these challenges by embracing uncertainty, managing stakeholder expectations effectively, addressing resistance to change head-on, balancing short-term results with long-term vision, and building high-performing teams.

By applying the principles outlined in Agile Rx, we can navigate these obstacles successfully and guide our teams toward greater agility and success. Let us embark on this journey together as we explore how being an agile leader is similar to being a medical doctor – both require constant learning, adaptability, empathy, and above all else - a commitment to the well-being of those under our care.

Of course, like doctors, we do make mistakes.

four

The 7 Agile Leader Mistakes - Mistake #1 - Practices Over Principles

As an agile leader, it is crucial to understand that simply jumping into the practices of agility without first grasping the underlying principles will hinder your journey toward true agility. This chapter explores Mistake #1: Placing practices over principles and emphasizes the importance of starting with the principles to foster a successful agile transformation.

In the world of agile, becoming truly agile as an individual, team, or organization cannot be achieved by solely focusing on the practices. It is essential to delve deep into the principles that serve as the foundation of agility.

Neglecting this step often leads to failure and leaves individuals wondering what went wrong. Even if you have mastered all the practices of popular frameworks like Scrum, without understanding and embracing the principles behind them, true agility will remain elusive.

To embark on a genuine agile transformation journey, it is vital to prioritize principles over practices. Agile is not merely about implementing certain methodologies or processes; it encompasses a mindset and way of thinking that permeates every aspect of your work.

A true transformation occurs when this mindset aligns with the guiding principles and becomes fully ingrained in your approach.

One common question that arises when discussing agile transformations is how long it takes to achieve such a shift. The answer may come as a surprise: one second.

True transformation happens in an instant when that proverbial lightbulb goes off in your mind, signaling your complete grasp and understanding of the agile mindset. It does not occur when you start doing agile things; rather it begins with adopting an agile way of thinking.

By prioritizing principles over practices, you lay a solid foundation for your agile journey. This approach simplifies navigating through complexity and fosters a deeper understanding of how agility can be applied effectively in various contexts.

When embarking on an agile transformation journey, don't rush straight into implementing practices blindly or treating them as mere checkboxes on a list. Instead, take the time to explore and internalize the principles that underpin agility. Understanding these principles allows you to adapt and tailor the practices to suit your specific needs, rather than blindly applying them without context.

One of the keys to success in agile transformation is embracing the mindset shift that accompanies the adoption of agile principles. This shift involves letting go of traditional, rigid ways of thinking and embracing flexibility, adaptability, collaboration, and continuous improvement. It requires a willingness to challenge established norms and experiment with new approaches.

The journey towards agility is not always straightforward. It requires patience, persistence, and a commitment to learning from both successes and failures along the way.

By prioritizing principles over practices, you set yourself on a path toward true agility—one that goes beyond surface-level changes and leads to a fundamental shift in mindset.

Placing practices over principles is a common pitfall in agile transformations. To truly embrace agility as an individual or organization, it is vital to prioritize understanding and internalizing the underlying principles first.

By doing so, you lay a strong foundation for successful practice implementation while fostering an agile mindset that permeates every aspect of your work. Remember that true transformation occurs in an instant when you grasp the agile mindset— it's not about starting with doing agile things but rather about embracing agile thinking from its core.

By adopting this approach throughout your journey towards agility, you will be better equipped to navigate complexity with confidence while continuously improving and adapting your practices for optimal results.

five

The 7 Agile Leader Mistakes - Mistake #2 - Not Recognizing The Problem To Be Solved

In the world of Agile leadership, one of the most critical mistakes a leader can make is not recognizing the problem that needs to be solved. It may seem like an obvious misstep, but many leaders fall into this trap, hindering their ability to drive effective change and improvement.

Agile leadership is not about blindly following trends or adopting Agile practices just because everyone else is doing it. It requires a deep understanding of the problems that exist within your organization and a commitment to addressing them head-on.

Before embarking on any Agile transformation journey, it is essential to take a step back and reflect on your current state. What are the biggest challenges your team or organization is facing? What are the bottlenecks that seem to hinder progress? Is quality suffering? Are you building the right things?

By asking these questions, you begin to uncover the true nature of the problems at hand. Sometimes, they may be obvious and straightforward. Other times, they may require a more in-depth analysis and investigation.

One common issue in organizations is continuous bottlenecks that impede workflow and slow down productivity. As an Agile leader, it is crucial to dig deeper and identify what truly causes these bottlenecks. Is it a lack of resources or skills? Are there inefficiencies in your processes? Or perhaps there are underlying communication issues within teams?

By recognizing these root causes, you can start implementing targeted solutions that address each specific problem area. For example, if it's a lack of resources causing bottlenecks, you could explore options like hiring additional team members or reallocating existing resources more effectively.

Another problem often encountered in organizations undergoing an Agile transformation is declining quality standards. Instead of simply accepting lower quality as an inevitable consequence of increased speed and agility, Agile leaders must investigate why quality has suffered in the first place.

Is it due to unrealistic deadlines being imposed on the team? Are there gaps in the testing process? Are there issues with collaboration and feedback loops between developers and testers?

Understanding the underlying reasons for compromised quality allows Agile leaders to implement strategies that address these issues directly. It could involve revisiting project timelines and setting more realistic expectations, investing in automated testing tools, or fostering a culture of collaboration and continuous improvement.

Lastly, Agile leaders must also ensure that the organization is building the right things. This requires a thorough examination of your product or service offerings to determine if they align with customer needs and business goals. If not, it's time to reassess your priorities.

Are you conducting regular market research and gathering customer feedback? Are you involving stakeholders early on in the development process to ensure their needs are met? By focusing on building the right things, Agile leaders can steer their teams towards delivering value-driven outcomes.

Recognizing the problem to be solved is paramount for Agile leaders. It is not enough to jump onto the Agile bandwagon without understanding why it is necessary or how it will address your organization's specific challenges.

Take time to reflect on your current state, identify bottlenecks, investigate declining quality standards, and reassess your product offerings. By doing so, you will lay a solid foundation for an effective Agile transformation that addresses real problems and drives meaningful change within your organization.

Remember: Agile leadership is about solving problems strategically rather than blindly implementing solutions.

six

The 7 Agile Leader Mistakes - Mistake #3 - Absent Leadership Support

Leadership is the cornerstone of any successful agile transformation. Without strong support and active involvement from leadership, the chances of a successful transformation are slim to none.

In this chapter, we will delve into the crucial role that leadership plays in driving and sustaining agility within an organization.

To begin with, it's important to clarify what support from leadership entails. It goes beyond merely allocating a budget or hiring external consultants. True support means being actively engaged in the transformation process and not shying away when challenges arise.

Agile transformations are not without their fair share of difficulties, and it is during these times that leadership support becomes even more critical.One of the key aspects leaders need to understand is that pain is an inevitable part of agile transformations.

However, this pain does not solely stem from embracing new methodologies; rather, it primarily arises from pre-existing issues within the organization that were previously concealed. In traditional project management approaches, problems often remain hidden until they eventually surface towards the end of a project cycle.

Agile flips this approach on its head by promoting transparency and early detection of issues. By doing so, organizations can address problems incrementally throughout iterations instead of waiting for them to accumulate over time. This shift may initially be uncomfortable for some individuals accustomed to concealing problems until they become too significant to ignore.

The solution lies in embracing failure as an opportunity for growth and improvement. When teams encounter setbacks or fail to meet expectations during their agile journey, leaders must provide unwavering support rather than assigning blame or finding fault.

By adopting a learning mindset and viewing failures as valuable lessons, teams can iterate upon their mistakes and continuously improve.

Leadership support also involves creating an environment where individuals feel safe sharing their concerns openly without fear of retribution or judgment. This psychological safety allows for honest conversations about challenges faced during the transformation process and fosters collaboration among team members.

When leaders actively encourage and listen to feedback, they empower their teams to voice their opinions and contribute towards finding innovative solutions.

Furthermore, leadership support extends beyond the immediate project team. It encompasses the entire organization, ensuring that all stakeholders understand and embrace the agile mindset. Leaders should communicate the vision for agile transformation clearly and consistently, aligning everyone towards a common goal. By doing so, they create a sense of purpose and direction that motivates individuals at all levels to actively participate in the transformation journey.

Leadership support is paramount for any successful agile transformation. It requires active involvement from leaders who are willing to weather the storm during challenging times and provide unwavering support to their teams. By embracing transparency, viewing failures as learning opportunities, fostering psychological safety, and aligning stakeholders towards a shared vision, leaders can pave the way for a truly agile organization.

Remember: Agile is not just about adopting new methodologies; it is about cultivating a culture of continuous improvement where teams thrive upon challenges and embrace change with open arms.

As an agile leader, your support can make all the difference in transforming your organization into an agile powerhouse capable of thriving in an ever-evolving business landscape.

So step up as an agile leader - be present, be supportive, be transformative!

seven

The 7 Agile Leader Mistakes - Mistake #4 - Lack of Agile Governance

In the world of agile leadership, there is often a misconception that there are different flavors or variations of agile. However, the truth is that there is only one flavor of agile, and it revolves around three core principles: value, adapting, and improving (See Chapter 1).

These principles reflect the essence of agility in any organization. When a leader dismisses or rejects the idea of being agile, they are essentially disregarding the importance of focusing on delivering value to their organization, adapting to changing circumstances, and continuously improving their ways of working.

While the fundamental principles remain constant across organizations, the paths taken to achieve agility may differ. This diversity in approaches necessitates the establishment of governance mechanisms to guide and monitor the implementation of agile practices. This need becomes even more critical for larger organizations with multiple divisions attempting to adopt agile from various sources and consultants.

The key objective of effective governance is not to dictate how an organization should implement agile but rather to provide guidance and prioritize goals. It creates a sense of continuity by ensuring that everyone involved understands what aspects are most important at any given moment.

To address this need for governance in an agile transformation journey, it is recommended to establish an Agile Center of Excellence (CoE). We will dive more into the concept of a CoE in a later chapter. This virtual organization consists of individuals with expertise in both agile methodologies and organizational dynamics. The CoE acts as a central hub for ensuring continuity throughout the transformation process.

One crucial responsibility of the CoE is developing an agile implementation roadmap that can adapt as needs change over time. This roadmap serves as a guiding document for teams across the organization by providing clarity on key milestones and deliverables. It outlines how different elements will be integrated into existing processes or structures while aligning them with organizational goals.

Furthermore, another vital role played by the CoE is identifying and addressing problems or impediments encountered during the transformation journey. By closely observing and investigating these issues within various departments or teams, they can design and propose suitable solutions. This proactive approach helps minimize disruptions and ensures a smooth transition to agile ways of working.

In addition, the CoE should actively seek out quick wins or low-hanging fruit opportunities to demonstrate the value of the transformation. By achieving incremental successes and tangible outcomes, they can build trust and credibility among those who may have doubts or reservations about embracing agility.

The Agile Center of Excellence should also serve as a knowledge hub, providing resources and support for individuals at all levels of the organization. This includes training programs, coaching sessions, workshops, and access to relevant tools or frameworks. By nurturing a learning culture within the organization, the CoE can foster continuous improvement and empower individuals to take ownership of their agile journeys.

To ensure effective governance, all voices within the organization must speak in unison concerning agile practices. The Agile Center of Excellence acts as a facilitator in aligning these diverse perspectives by fostering collaboration and encouraging open communication channels. This unity enables organizations to leverage collective wisdom while still allowing for flexibility based on specific needs or contexts.

Successful governance in an agile transformation requires the establishment of an Agile Center of Excellence that acts as a guiding force throughout the journey. This virtual organization ensures continuity by developing an adaptive implementation roadmap and addressing organizational impediments proactively.

Demonstrating tangible results through incremental success stories builds trust among skeptics while fostering a culture of continuous learning. With effective governance in place, organizations can navigate their agile transformations more smoothly while maximizing value delivery and adaptability.

eight

The 7 Agile Leader Mistakes - Mistake #5 - Only Following the Rules

Know When to Pivot

I get it. We are told our entire lives not to break the rules. This is generally true, but when it comes to being an Agile leader, there are times when you need to just break some rules and ignore certain advice. Agile is not one size fits all, and blindly following the rules can lead to ineffective results.

You might have taken an Agile course or heard an Agile coach or consultant tell you that you, "should do this," or "you should never do that." It's easy to become a stickler about it and insist that this is how Agile tells us to do it. But I'm here to tell you: stop! Don't be afraid to question the rules and advice that you come across in your Agile journey.

As a consultant myself, I understand the irony of telling you what you should be doing. But I want to emphasize that blindly following the rules can be a mistake. If you find yourself following certain rules or advice, but the results feel more painful than they should, then it's time for a change.

In medicine, doctors don't simply follow a set of predetermined guidelines for every patient. They assess each case and make decisions based on what they observe and learn from their patients' symptoms. Similarly, as an Agile leader, you must treat the symptoms themselves rather than just adhering strictly to what you've heard or learned.

The key is knowing when to pivot and where to pivot to. Pivoting means being open-minded and willing to adapt your approach when necessary. It means recognizing when something isn't working and having the courage to try something different.

But how do you know when it's time? How do you know if following certain rules is hindering your progress rather than helping? The answer lies in observation and paying attention.

Take a step back and evaluate the outcomes of your actions. Are they aligning with the goals and values of Agile? Are they bringing about the desired results? If not, it's a clear sign that something needs to change. Don't be afraid to experiment and try new approaches. Agile is all about continuous improvement, and that includes being willing to break free from rigid rules when necessary.

Trust your instincts as a leader and be open to alternative paths that may lead to better outcomes. Of course, this doesn't mean you should disregard all rules and advice without thought. It's important to strike a balance between following established principles and being flexible enough to adapt as needed.

Use your judgment and consider the context of your specific situation. Remember, Agile is about embracing change and learning from experience. It's about finding what works best for your team or organization rather than blindly conforming to one prescribed way of doing things.

Only Following the Rules, can hinder your Agile transformation journey. Don't be afraid to question the rules you come across or the advice you receive. Be willing to pivot when necessary, knowing when it's time for a change in approach. Embrace experimentation and continuous improvement, always keeping in mind that Agile is not one size fits all.

As an Agile leader, your role is not just about following rules; it's about guiding your team toward better outcomes through flexibility, adaptation, and a willingness to challenge the status quo.

Stay agile in both mindset and action, knowing when to pivot will ultimately lead you towards success in your Agile transformation journey.

nine

The 7 Agile Leader Mistakes - Mistake #6 - A Bad Taste

Have you ever tried something new and found it so unpleasant that you never wanted to try it again? This happens quite often in the world of Agile. I have come across countless individuals who have developed a strong dislike for Agile, to the point where even hearing the word makes them cringe.

There are generally two reasons behind this aversion.

The first reason is that some team members prefer working in isolation, within their silo. They may be highly skilled and dedicated workers, but when placed on an Agile team, they become uncomfortable. The transparency and collaboration that are integral to Agile practices can be unsettling for them.

They may fear that their shortcomings will be exposed or simply dislike the idea of working closely with others. While this reason is unfortunate, it is also understandable to some extent.

The second reason is also quite common. Some individuals have had previous experiences with Agile at another organization that were so unpleasant, they left a lasting bad taste.

These experiences may have involved pain, frustration, and a general sense of not wanting to go to work every day. In all likelihood, these organizations made one or more of the seven mistakes we have discussed in this book. They may have implemented various Agile practices without truly understanding the underlying principles or used Agile just for the sake of it without addressing specific problems they were trying to solve.

AGILE RX: A PRESCRIPTION TO GUIDE AGILE LEADERS

Alternatively, they may have lacked true Agile leadership or governance or simply adhered rigidly to a set of rules learned in a short Scrum class. Such experiences will inevitably lead to bitterness towards Agile.

These individuals were never exposed to an environment where Agile truly thrives. If you find yourself in this situation, I encourage you to reflect on your experience and consider whether you or your organization fell into any of those seven mistakes mentioned earlier.

If you did make those mistakes, take action now and rid yourself of that bad taste! As a leader within your organization, it is your responsibility to help others avoid making the same errors. Use your own negative experience as a learning opportunity and guide those around you towards a better understanding of Agile.

Even if you did not have a bad taste from previous encounters with Agile, chances are you will encounter someone who did or will in the future. When you come across such individuals, my advice remains the same: lead by example. Share with them what you have learned and demonstrate why Agile can indeed work when implemented correctly.

The solution lies in disregarding that bad taste because what you experienced before was not true Agile. Learn from your past experiences and share that knowledge with others, so they too can understand the potential of Agile when applied effectively.

It is common for people to develop a dislike for Agile due to either personal discomfort or negative past experiences. However, by addressing the seven mistakes we have discussed throughout this book and leading by example, we can overcome these challenges and create an environment where Agile thrives.

Let us learn from our mistakes and help others do the same so that together we can embrace the true power of being an Agile leader.

Remember: Ignore that bad taste; it's time to reshape our understanding of Agile and share our newfound knowledge with others.

ten

The 7 Agile Leader Mistakes - Mistake #7 - Can't Let Go, Not Letting It Flow

Change is hard, especially when you have been doing something a certain way for a long time. But to be successful as an Agile leader, you need to let go of old habits and embrace new ways of thinking.

This chapter explores the importance of letting go and allowing things to flow naturally. As a leader, your entire career may have revolved around meeting time-based goals. The focus was always on getting things done on time and ensuring your team accomplished their work within the designated schedule.

However, simply completing tasks on time does not guarantee success. True success lies in building the right things, building them correctly, and delivering value to the customer. As an Agile leader, it is essential to shift your focus from meeting deadlines to prioritizing customer happiness.

When asked about the most important metric to track, many people expect a complex answer involving various performance indicators. However, the truth is simple: customer happiness should be your primary metric. When your customers are happy with what you deliver, all other metrics become irrelevant. Therefore, it is crucial to let go of outdated notions of success and instead prioritize delivering value that satisfies your customers' needs.

Embracing Agile principles means allowing things to flow naturally, even if it feels uncomfortable at first. In this new world of agility, authority shifts towards where knowledge resides rather than being concentrated in one individual or position. This can be disconcerting for those accustomed to traditional hierarchical structures but embracing this change will ultimately lead to better outcomes.

AGILE RX: A PRESCRIPTION TO GUIDE AGILE LEADERS

Traditional approaches to project management were developed in a task-based world where time estimates and structured plans worked effectively. However, when dealing with knowledge work such as software development or complex problem-solving tasks that involve uncertainty and unknowns, these traditional methods fall short.

Agile methodologies emerged as a response to the limitations of traditional approaches in dealing with knowledge work. They offer flexible frameworks that adapt to the ever-changing requirements and complexities of such tasks. By embracing Agile, you are acknowledging the need for a different approach—one that allows for continuous improvement, adaptation, and embracing uncertainty.

Letting go of old habits can be uncomfortable. It may feel unnatural at first to relinquish control and embrace a more fluid way of working. However, by doing so, you unlock the potential for innovation and creativity within your team. Embracing change allows you to tap into the collective knowledge and expertise of your team members.

The key is to stay focused on delivering the highest value while adapting with minimal resistance. This requires continuously improving your processes and practices based on feedback and learning from each iteration. As an Agile leader, it is your responsibility to foster an environment that encourages experimentation, collaboration, and growth.

Can't Let Go: Not Letting It Flow—is a common pitfall for leaders transitioning to Agile methodologies. However, by embracing change, letting go of outdated notions of success based solely on meeting deadlines, and allowing things to flow naturally in an agile environment, you open up new possibilities for growth and success.

Remember that agility is not just about following a set of rules or adopting specific practices—it is a mindset shift that requires continuous learning and adaptation. By letting go of old habits, embracing uncertainty, prioritizing customer happiness above all else, and focusing on delivering value through flexible processes that adapt with ease—Agile leaders can truly excel in their roles.

So take a deep breath—let go—and let it flow!

eleven

Building a Strong Foundation

The Agile Leader's Toolkit

In the fast-paced and ever-changing world of modern organizations, leadership plays a critical role in driving success. Agile leadership, with its emphasis on adaptability, collaboration, and continuous improvement, has emerged as a key prescription for achieving organizational growth.

In this chapter, we will explore the core principles of agility in leadership and delve into the essential toolkit that every Agile Leader should possess.

Understanding the Core Principles of Agility in Leadership:

Agile leadership is rooted in a growth mindset that embraces change and uncertainty as opportunities for learning and improvement. It requires leaders to let go of traditional hierarchical structures and instead foster an environment of collaboration and teamwork. By encouraging open communication, and experimentation, and embracing failure as a learning opportunity, Agile Leaders create an atmosphere where creativity thrives.

Cultivating Self-Awareness and Emotional Intelligence:

Self-awareness is an essential trait for any leader but is particularly crucial for Agile Leaders. By understanding their strengths, weaknesses, values, and triggers, they can better navigate complex situations with empathy and emotional intelligence. This self-awareness allows them to connect with team members on a deeper level by understanding their needs and motivations.

Mastering Effective Communication Skills:

Communication lies at the heart of successful agile leadership. As an Agile Leader interacts with diverse teams consisting of individuals from different backgrounds or departments within an organization, mastering effective communication skills becomes imperative. Clear articulation of goals, expectations, feedback mechanisms are crucial to foster collaboration among team members.

Leveraging Technology to Enhance Agility:

In today's digital age, technology serves as a powerful tool for enhancing agility in decision-making processes. Agile Leaders leverage technological solutions such as project management software or collaborative platforms to streamline workflows and enable real-time communication across distributed teams. By harnessing technology effectively within their toolkit, they can make informed decisions quickly while adapting to changing circumstances.

Diagnosis - Identifying Organizational Pains with Precision:

Just as a medical doctor diagnoses a patient's ailments, Agile Leaders diagnose organizational challenges with precision. They employ agile frameworks such as Scrum or Kanban to assess the health of an organization. Regular retrospectives and visual boards enable them to gather data, metrics, and feedback essential for accurate diagnosis. Additionally, Agile Leaders utilize empathy and active listening techniques to uncover underlying issues that may not be immediately apparent.

Prescribing Solutions - Implementing Agile Practices for Growth:

Once the diagnosis is complete, Agile Leaders prescribe solutions by implementing agile practices tailored to address the identified challenges. They introduce iterative planning, sprints, or daily stand-ups to foster transparency and collaboration among team members. Prioritization techniques such as the MoSCoW method or impact-effort matrix help them allocate resources effectively. By applying lean principles and promoting continuous learning through experimentation, feedback loops, and retrospectives, they create an environment conducive to growth.

Nurturing a Culture of Agility - Leading by Example:

AGILE RX: A PRESCRIPTION TO GUIDE AGILE LEADERS

Agile Leadership extends beyond individual practices; it encompasses fostering a culture of agility within an organization. Agile Leaders create safe environments that encourage risk-taking, innovation, and continuous improvement. By fostering psychological safety within teams through open communication channels and constructive feedback mechanisms, they empower individuals to contribute their best ideas without fear of judgment or reprisal.

Overcoming Resistance - Dealing with The Organizational Immune System:

Change is often met with resistance in organizations - the immune system that seeks to maintain the status quo. Agile Leaders identify common sources of resistance by engaging stakeholders through effective communication plans. Utilizing change management frameworks helps them navigate challenges while addressing individual concerns related to agile transformation empathetically. Building a coalition of change agents strengthens their ability to champion the agile journey throughout the organization.

Thriving in the Agile Era - Sustaining Agility for Long-Term Success:

Agile Leadership is not a temporary fix but rather requires sustained effort. Agile Leaders establish mechanisms for continuous learning, improvement, and adaptation to ensure long-term success. They scale agility across the organization by adopting frameworks like SAFe° or LeSS to align teams and improve collaboration. Nurturing leadership pipelines that cultivate future Agile Leaders ensures the sustainability of agile practices within the organization.

Furthermore, Agile Leaders embrace agile principles beyond the workplace into their personal lives, leading by example and inspiring others to do the same.

Conclusion:

Building a strong foundation is essential for an Agile Leader's journey towards success. By understanding the core principles of agility in leadership, cultivating self-awareness and emotional intelligence, mastering effective communication skills, leveraging technology effectively, diagnosing organizational challenges with precision, prescribing appropriate solutions, nurturing a culture of agility, overcoming resistance to change, and sustaining agility for long-term success; Agile Leaders can transform their organizations into thriving ecosystems that embrace change as an opportunity for growth.

twelve

Diagnosis

Identifying Organizational Pains with Precision

One of the key responsibilities of Agile Leaders is to diagnose organizational pains with precision. Just like a medical doctor, an Agile Leader must possess the ability to analyze symptoms, gather information, and uncover underlying issues that hinder an organization's growth.

This chapter explores various methods and techniques that Agile Leaders can employ to accurately diagnose organizational challenges.

Methods for Assessing Organizational Health

To effectively assess the health of an organization, Agile Leaders can utilize agile frameworks such as Scrum or Kanban. These frameworks provide valuable tools for conducting regular retrospectives or using visual boards to track progress. By encouraging teams to reflect on their work and identify areas for improvement, Agile Leaders gain insights into potential pain points within the organization.

Furthermore, analyzing data, metrics, and feedback is crucial in diagnosing organizational challenges accurately. By collecting objective data regarding team performance, customer satisfaction levels, and project outcomes, leaders can gain a comprehensive understanding of where problems lie. This data-driven approach helps identify patterns and trends that may be contributing to inefficiencies or obstacles.

Uncovering Underlying Issues Through Empathy and Active Listening

While data analysis provides valuable insights into organizational challenges, it is equally important for Agile Leaders to engage in empathetic communication with their teams. By actively listening and seeking to understand team members' perspectives and concerns, leaders can uncover underlying issues that may not be immediately apparent through quantitative analysis alone.

Empathy allows leaders to connect on a deeper level with their teams' experiences and emotions. It enables them to address not just the symptoms but also the root causes of organizational pains. Through empathetic conversations and open dialogue, Agile Leaders create a safe space for team members to express their thoughts freely.

Utilizing active listening techniques further enhances this process by ensuring leaders truly hear what their team members are saying without judgment or interruption. Active listening involves fully focusing on the speaker, asking clarifying questions, and summarizing key points to demonstrate understanding. This approach encourages team members to share their perspectives openly, leading to a more accurate diagnosis of organizational challenges.

Case Study: Applying Agile Diagnosis

To illustrate the process of diagnosing organizational challenges, let's consider a fictional company called Tech Solutions Inc. The company has been experiencing a decline in customer satisfaction ratings and an increase in project delays.

The Agile Leader at Tech Solutions Inc., Sarah, decides to apply various agile diagnosis methods.

Sarah starts by conducting retrospectives with her teams to gather insights into recurring issues and potential solutions. Through these retrospectives, she discovers that communication breakdown between teams is a significant contributor to project delays and customer dissatisfaction.

Utilizing data analysis techniques, Sarah examines project metrics and feedback from customers. She uncovers that the misalignment between customer expectations and deliverables is causing dissatisfaction.

Additionally, she notices that there is limited cross-functional collaboration within the organization. Sarah then engages in empathetic conversations with team members from different departments. Through active listening and open dialogue, she discovers that some employees feel hesitant to speak up about their concerns for fear of retribution or being seen as complainers.

Based on her observations and findings, Sarah diagnoses two underlying issues within Tech Solutions Inc.: poor interdepartmental communication and a lack of psychological safety among employees.

By accurately diagnosing these problems through agile methods such as retrospectives, data analysis, empathy, and active listening techniques, Sarah can now move forward with prescribing appropriate solutions for organizational growth

Just as doctors diagnose patients' illnesses by analyzing symptoms and gathering information through tests or examinations, Agile Leaders diagnose organizational pains through methods like retrospectives, data analysis, and empathetic conversations.

The book title suggests that Agile Leadership requires a similar level of precision and attention to detail as practicing medicine. Both involve identifying symptoms, analyzing data, engaging with individuals, and ultimately prescribing solutions for growth or healing.

By exploring the diagnosis phase in this chapter, readers gain a deeper understanding of how Agile Leaders can effectively assess an organization's health and uncover underlying issues. This knowledge enables them to make informed decisions and guide their teams towards long-term success.

Conclusion

Diagnosing organizational pains with precision is a crucial responsibility of an Agile Leader. By utilizing agile frameworks, analyzing data, metrics, and feedback, as well as employing empathy and active listening techniques, leaders can accurately identify underlying issues within their organizations.

In the next chapter, we will delve into prescribing solutions for organizational growth based on the insights gained during the diagnosis phase.

thirteen

Prescribing Solutions

Implementing Agile Practices for Growth

As an Agile Leader, your role is not only to diagnose organizational challenges, as noted in the previous chapter but also to prescribe effective solutions for growth and improvement.

This chapter will delve into the importance of implementing agile practices and explore various techniques that can be used to foster agility within your organization.

Introducing agile practices is like administering the right medicine to a patient. Just as a doctor carefully prescribes medications based on the patient's symptoms and condition, an Agile Leader must understand the specific needs of their organization before implementing Agile practices.

By doing so, you can ensure that you are addressing the root causes of organizational challenges rather than merely treating the symptoms.

One of the fundamental principles of agility is iterative planning. Instead of creating rigid long-term plans that may become outdated in a rapidly changing environment, Agile Leaders encourage their teams to break down projects into smaller, manageable iterations known as sprints. These sprints allow for continuous feedback and adjustment, ensuring that teams stay on track towards their goals.

To prioritize tasks effectively within these iterations, Agile Leaders often use techniques such as the MoSCoW[1] method or impact-effort matrix. The MoSCoW method helps identify tasks based on their Must-haves, Should-haves, Could-haves, and Won't-haves categories.

AGILE RX: A PRESCRIPTION TO GUIDE AGILE LEADERS

By prioritizing work based on its significance and urgency, teams can focus on delivering high-value outcomes first.

Additionally, applying lean principles can help eliminate waste and optimize processes within your organization. Just as doctors strive to reduce unnecessary procedures or treatments that do not contribute to healing patients' ailments efficiently, Agile Leaders aim to streamline workflows by identifying and eliminating activities that do not add value or hinder productivity.

Promoting continuous learning is another vital aspect of implementing agile practices for growth. Through experimentation, feedback loops, and regular retrospectives – where teams reflect on past experiences – organizations can identify areas for improvement and make necessary adjustments accordingly. Agile Leaders encourage their teams to learn from both successes and failures, fostering a culture of continuous improvement and adaptation.

Supporting self-managed teams is crucial for agile success. Agile Leaders empower their teams with autonomy, allowing them to make decisions and take ownership of their work. Just like how doctors trust their patients to manage their health through lifestyle changes or medication adherence, Agile Leaders trust their teams to deliver results by providing guidance and support when needed.

By implementing these agile practices, you are not only prescribing solutions for your organization's growth but also nurturing a culture of agility. As an Agile Leader, leading by example is essential in cultivating this mindset within your team.

Creating a safe environment that encourages risk-taking, innovation and continuous improvement is paramount. By fostering psychological safety within teams – where individuals feel comfortable sharing ideas, asking questions, and providing constructive feedback – you can unleash the full potential of your organization's collective intelligence.

Trust and transparency are also vital aspects of leading by example. Agile Leaders practice servant leadership by putting the needs of their team first and supporting them in achieving their goals. By building trust through open communication, transparency in decision-making processes, and actively listening to the concerns and ideas of team members, you can foster an environment that promotes collaboration and innovation.

In addition to this, embracing failure as a learning opportunity plays a significant role in nurturing agility within your organization. Just like how doctors understand that not every treatment will be successful but use those experiences to refine future approaches, Agile Leaders encourage teams to embrace failure as part of the learning process. By reframing failure as an opportunity for growth rather than punishment or blame, organizations can create an atmosphere where experimentation and innovation thrive.

Lastly, recognizing and celebrating achievements are essential motivators for sustaining agility in the long run. As an Agile Leader, acknowledging individual contributions as well as team accomplishments helps boost morale and encourages continued excellence. By celebrating milestones along the agile journey together, you create a sense of shared purpose and commitment to continuous improvement.

Implementing agile practices is like prescribing the right medicine for your organization's growth. By introducing iterative planning, prioritizing tasks effectively, applying lean principles, promoting continuous learning, supporting self-managed teams, and nurturing a culture of agility through leading by example, you can prescribe the optimal solutions for organizational success.

Just as doctors adapt their treatment plans based on patient feedback and changing conditions, Agile Leaders must continuously assess and adjust their agile practices to ensure long-term agility and resilience in the face of evolving challenges.

The next chapter will explore overcoming resistance within organizations during an agile transformation – likening it to dealing with an "organizational immune system" that resists change. We will discuss strategies for addressing resistance and building a coalition of change agents who can champion the agile journey within your organization.

1 Clegg, Dai; Barker, Richard (1994). *Case Method Fast-Track: A RAD Approach*. Addison-Wesley. ISBN 978-0-201-62432-8

35

Overcoming Resistance

Dealing with the Organizational Immune System

In the journey towards agility, organizations often encounter resistance that can impede progress and hinder successful transformation. Similar to how a body's immune system reacts to foreign substances, organizations have their own "immune system" that responds to change.

In this chapter, we delve into the challenges of overcoming resistance and provide strategies for navigating through these obstacles. Just as a doctor must address the body's immune response to administer treatment effectively, an Agile Leader must understand and mitigate organizational resistance to drive lasting change.

Identifying Common Sources of Resistance:

Resistance is a natural reaction when individuals are confronted with change. It can stem from various sources such as fear of the unknown, loss of control, or perceived threats to one's status or competence. By recognizing these common sources of resistance within organizations, Agile Leaders can proactively address them.

One effective strategy is stakeholder engagement. Identifying key stakeholders and involving them early in the transformation process fosters ownership and reduces resistance. Clear communication plans are crucial in managing expectations and ensuring transparency throughout the journey. By openly discussing fears and concerns while emphasizing the benefits of agility, leaders can create a shared understanding that eases resistance.

Utilizing Change Management Frameworks:

AGILE RX: A PRESCRIPTION TO GUIDE AGILE LEADERS

Change management frameworks provide structure and guidance for managing organizational change effectively. These frameworks help leaders navigate through challenges by providing a systematic approach tailored to the unique needs of each organization.

One such framework is ADKAR[1] (Awareness, Desire, Knowledge, Ability, Reinforcement). It emphasizes addressing individual concerns at each stage of change by building awareness about why agility is necessary, fostering a desire for its benefits through effective communication, providing knowledge through training programs, developing skills required for agile practices, and reinforcing new behaviors consistently.

Addressing Individual Concerns:

Individual concerns play a significant role in organizational resistance. Agile Leaders must take time to listen actively to employees' apprehensions while empathizing with their fears and frustrations. By addressing these concerns openly and honestly, leaders can alleviate resistance and build trust.

In addition, fostering a culture of psychological safety is vital. Creating an environment where individuals feel safe to voice their opinions, ask questions, and share ideas without fear of judgment or retribution enables open communication and helps overcome resistance.

Building a Coalition of Change Agents:

To drive successful agile transformations, Agile Leaders need allies who champion the change within the organization. Building a coalition of change agents allows for distributed leadership and increases the likelihood of adoption across teams.

Identifying early adopters who embrace agility and empowering them to lead by example can significantly influence others' perception of change. These change agents play a crucial role in sharing success stories, providing mentorship, and addressing concerns from their peers, thus breaking down resistance barriers.

Navigating Resistance through Communication:

Effective communication is essential when dealing with resistance. Agile Leaders should communicate not only the "what" but also the "why" behind organizational changes. Explaining how agility aligns with the organization's vision and goals enhances understanding and reduces uncertainty.

Moreover, active listening becomes an invaluable tool during times of resistance. By genuinely hearing employees' perspectives without judgment or interruption, leaders can gain valuable insights that help tailor solutions to specific challenges.

Conclusion:

Overcoming resistance is an integral part of any transformational journey towards becoming an Agile Leader. Understanding common sources of resistance within organizations allows leaders to develop strategies that address individual concerns while engaging stakeholders throughout the process. By utilizing change management frameworks, fostering psychological safety, building coalitions of change agents, and communicating effectively, Agile Leaders can navigate through resistance barriers successfully.

Just as doctors must navigate patients' immune responses to administer treatments effectively for better health outcomes, Agile Leaders must navigate organizational immune systems for successful agile transformations that lead to long-term organizational health and sustainability in today's ever-changing business landscape.

By embracing the challenge of overcoming resistance head-on, Agile Leaders can pave the way for a culture of agility that drives innovation, and growth, and ultimately sets their organizations on a path to thrive in the Agile Era.

1 - https://www.prosci.com/methodology/adkar

fifteen

Nurturing a Culture of Agility

Leading By Example

In the previous chapters, we explored the foundations of Agile Leadership, diagnosed organizational pains with precision, and prescribed solutions for growth. Now, we delve into the critical aspect of nurturing a culture of agility within organizations. Just like a medical doctor leads by example in promoting health and well-being, an Agile Leader plays a crucial role in shaping the culture that fosters innovation, collaboration, and continuous improvement.

Creating a Safe Environment:

To cultivate agility within teams, an Agile Leader must create a safe environment where individuals feel comfortable taking risks and exploring new ideas. Psychological safety is key to encouraging open communication, idea-sharing, and constructive feedback. By actively listening to team members' concerns and valuing their contributions without judgment or repercussion, leaders can build trust and transparency.

Leading with Servant Leadership:

Agile Leaders practice servant leadership by shifting their focus from authority to serving their teams. This approach enables them to empower individuals with autonomy while providing guidance when needed. By removing obstacles that hinder progress and supporting self-managed teams in decision-making processes, leaders foster accountability and ownership among team members.

Embracing Failure as a Learning Opportunity:

In an agile culture, failure is not seen as something negative but rather as an opportunity for growth. Agile Leaders encourage a growth mindset where individuals view setbacks as valuable learning experiences. By openly discussing failures and extracting lessons from them instead of assigning blame or punishment, leaders create an atmosphere that promotes continuous improvement.

Fostering Continuous Improvement:

Agility thrives on continuous learning and adaptation. Agile Leaders establish mechanisms for ongoing improvement by implementing feedback loops throughout the organization. Regular retrospectives provide opportunities to reflect on past performance and identify areas for enhancement. Through iterative experiments and adjustments based on feedback received from both internal stakeholders and customers alike, leaders drive innovation while maintaining alignment with organizational goals.

Recognizing Achievements:

Celebrating achievements is essential in nurturing a culture of agility. Agile Leaders acknowledge and appreciate the efforts and accomplishments of individuals and teams. By publicly recognizing successes, leaders inspire motivation and enthusiasm among team members. This recognition can take various forms, such as verbal praise during team meetings, rewards or incentives for exceptional performance, or even sharing success stories within the organization to inspire others.

Throughout this book, you may have noticed that we draw parallels between the roles of an Agile Leader and a medical doctor. Just as doctors lead by example in promoting health and well-being for their patients, Agile Leaders play a crucial role in creating a culture that fosters growth, innovation, and collaboration within organizations.

By adopting principles from the medical profession such as creating a safe environment, practicing servant leadership, embracing failure as a learning opportunity, fostering continuous improvement, and recognizing achievements – leaders can prescribe an agile treatment plan for their organizations' success.

Conclusion:

AGILE RX: A PRESCRIPTION TO GUIDE AGILE LEADERS

Nurturing a culture of agility is vital for long-term organizational success in today's fast-paced business landscape. By creating safe environments where individuals feel empowered to take risks and share ideas openly while fostering continuous learning through experimentation and feedback loops, Agile Leaders lay the foundation for sustained growth. Embracing failure as an opportunity for growth while recognizing achievements further motivates teams to strive for excellence. In doing so, leaders set an example that inspires others to embrace agility not only at work but also in their personal lives.

As we look towards the future of Agile Leadership, it is important to continue evolving with emerging practices and trends that will shape organizations' ability to adapt successfully in this ever-changing world.

sixteen

Thriving in the Agile Era

Sustaining Agility for Long-Term Success

As organizations continue to embrace agility, it is essential to understand how to sustain and thrive in the Agile era. This chapter explores the mechanisms and strategies that Agile Leaders can employ to ensure long-term success.

Just as medical doctors continuously adapt their practices to advancements in healthcare, Agile Leaders must evolve their leadership approach to meet the changing needs of their organizations.

Establishing Mechanisms for Continuous Learning, Improvement, and Adaptation:

Agile Leaders recognize that learning is an ongoing process. They establish mechanisms within their organizations that foster continuous improvement and adaptation. This includes promoting a culture of curiosity and experimentation where individuals are encouraged to question existing practices and explore new ways of working.

To facilitate continuous learning, Agile Leaders implement regular knowledge-sharing sessions such as lunch-and-learn sessions or communities of practice where employees can exchange ideas and experiences. They also encourage cross-functional collaboration to harness diverse perspectives and insights.

Furthermore, Agile Leaders leverage feedback loops throughout the organization. They collect feedback from customers, employees, and stakeholders regularly and use this information to drive improvements. By embracing a growth mindset, they view feedback as an opportunity for growth rather than criticism.

AGILE RX: A PRESCRIPTION TO GUIDE AGILE LEADERS

Scaling Agility Across the Organization:

Agile transformation is not limited to individual teams but should be scaled across the entire organization for maximum impact. Agile Leaders understand this need for scalability and employ frameworks like SAFe (Scaled Agile Framework) or LeSS (Large-Scale Scrum) to enable agility at scale.

These frameworks guide how multiple teams can collaborate effectively while maintaining alignment with organizational goals. They introduce concepts such as value streams, program increments, or release trains that enable coordinated planning across teams.

Additionally, Agile Leaders focus on establishing clear communication channels between teams at different levels of the organization. Regular synchronization meetings ensure transparency in progress towards shared objectives while fostering collaboration between teams.

Nurturing Leadership Pipelines:

Agile Leaders recognize the importance of developing future Agile Leaders within their organizations. They understand that sustainable agility requires a strong leadership pipeline to drive change and inspire others.

To nurture leadership, Agile Leaders provide opportunities for growth and development. They identify potential leaders and offer them mentorship, coaching, or training programs tailored to their needs. By investing in the development of emerging leaders, Agile Leaders ensure a continuous supply of individuals who can effectively guide agile transformations and lead teams in an ever-changing environment.

Embracing Agile Principles Beyond the Workplace:

I always emphasize that being an Agile Leader is not limited to professional life but extends into personal life as well. Just as medical doctors prioritize their well-being to better care for others, Agile Leaders understand the importance of personal agility.

Agile Leaders embrace agile principles in their personal lives by seeking balance, practicing self-care, and fostering continuous learning outside of work. They understand that by taking care of themselves physically, mentally, and emotionally, they can bring their best selves to the workplace.

The Future of Agile Leadership - Evolving Trends and Emerging Practices:

As the business landscape continues to evolve rapidly, so does the practice of Agile Leadership. In this section, we explore emerging trends and practices that hold promise for future success.

One such trend is the integration of artificial intelligence (AI) into agile practices. AI-powered tools can help analyze data more efficiently, automate repetitive tasks, or even predict potential bottlenecks in project delivery.

Additionally, as organizations become more globalized and remote work becomes increasingly prevalent, virtual collaboration tools are gaining importance. Agile Leaders need to adapt their communication strategies accordingly to maintain effective teamwork across geographically dispersed teams.

Conclusion:

Thriving in the Agile era requires continuous learning, and scalability across the organization while nurturing future leaders through effective leadership pipelines. It also involves embracing agility beyond work boundaries and staying abreast with evolving trends and practices.

Just like medical doctors, Agile Leaders understand that sustained success comes from a commitment to ongoing learning, adapting to change, and prioritizing the well-being of both themselves and their teams. By applying the principles discussed in this chapter, Agile Leaders can ensure they remain at the forefront of leadership practices in today's dynamic business environment.

We have, so far, explored how Agile Leadership and medical practice share similarities in terms of adaptability, continuous improvement, and diagnosing problems for growth. This chapter has provided insights into sustaining agility for long-term success by establishing mechanisms for continuous learning, scaling agility across the organization, nurturing leadership pipelines, embracing agile principles beyond work boundaries, and exploring emerging trends. As we continue this book, let us continue our journey as Agile Leaders with an unwavering commitment to agility and a passion for making a positive impact in our organizations.

seventeen

Fail to Succeed

Failure is an inherent part of the journey towards success. In the world of Agile leadership, this concept holds as well. Agile Leaders need to embrace failure as a stepping stone towards growth and improvement. This chapter delves into the importance of failing to succeed, drawing inspiration from various innovations in science and medicine throughout history.

Throughout centuries, scientists and medical professionals have pushed the boundaries of knowledge through relentless experimentation and perseverance. Countless innovators have faced repeated failures before achieving groundbreaking success. One such example is Thomas Edison, who famously stated, "I have not failed. I've just found 10,000 ways that won't work."

His tireless pursuit of creating a practical electric light bulb involved numerous setbacks and disappointments before he finally succeeded.

Agile Leaders can draw valuable lessons from these stories of resilience and determination. When faced with failure, it is crucial to view it as an opportunity for learning rather than a setback. Each failure provides valuable insights that can guide future actions and decisions.

One important aspect highlighted in this chapter is the necessity for continuous improvement. Agile Leaders understand that stagnation leads to mediocrity, whereas embracing failure fosters growth and innovation within their teams or organizations. By encouraging experimentation without fear of failure, leaders create an environment where individuals feel empowered to take risks and learn from their mistakes.

After experiencing a setback or failure, Agile Leaders should take certain actions to ensure they extract maximum value from the experience:

1. Embrace Reflection:

46

Instead of dwelling on negative emotions or blaming external factors for failure, Agile Leaders should encourage self-reflection among themselves and their team members. By examining what went wrong objectively, they can identify areas for improvement and develop strategies to overcome future challenges.

2. Encourage Collaboration:

Failure should not be seen as an individual's burden but rather as a shared experience within a team or organization. Agile Leaders foster collaboration by creating a culture where team members can openly discuss failures, share insights, and collectively brainstorm solutions. This collaborative approach not only strengthens bonds but also promotes a learning mindset throughout the entire organization.

3. Foster Psychological Safety:

Agile Leaders understand that failure can be intimidating and may discourage individuals from taking risks. To counteract this, they prioritize psychological safety within their teams. By creating an environment where team members feel safe to voice their ideas, ask questions, and admit mistakes without fear of judgment or retribution, leaders encourage innovation and experimentation.

4. Iterate and Adapt:

Failure is not the end but rather a stepping stone towards success. Agile Leaders emphasize the importance of iteration and adaptation in response to failure. By continuously refining strategies based on lessons learned, leaders guide their teams toward improved performance and greater resilience.

5. Celebrate Progress:

Recognizing small victories along the way is crucial for maintaining motivation in the face of failure. Agile Leaders acknowledge the progress made even during challenging times to keep spirits high and inspire their teams to persevere.

By embracing failure as an opportunity for growth, Agile Leaders cultivate resilience within themselves and their teams. They create an environment that encourages continuous improvement through experimentation, collaboration, reflection, psychological safety, iteration, and celebrating progress.

This chapter highlighted how failing is an integral part of the journey towards success for Agile Leaders. Drawing inspiration from historical examples of innovation in science and medicine, it emphasizes the importance of learning from failures to drive continuous improvement. By following specific actions after experiencing setbacks or failures, Agile Leaders foster a culture of resilience and innovation within their organizations.

eighteen

Objectives and OKRs

Objectives and Key Results (OKRs) play a crucial role in the success of any organization. In this chapter, we will explore what objectives are, how they should be written, and how OKRs can be used to measure their progress. We will also delve into the importance of assigning business value to features and epics during the planning phase and measuring their actual value once implemented.

To begin with, let's understand what objectives are and why they matter. Objectives are clear and concise statements that outline specific goals an organization aims to achieve within a given timeframe. They provide direction, focus, and alignment for teams working towards a common purpose. However, writing effective objectives is not always an easy task.

One common challenge many organizations face is even getting to a point where objectives are written. People often struggle with articulating their goals clearly or fail to understand how these goals relate to the overall strategy of the organization. Therefore, it is crucial to establish a framework for writing objectives that ensures they are meaningful and measurable.

When crafting objectives, it is important to follow some key principles:

1. **Specificity:**

Objectives should be specific rather than vague or broad. They must clearly state what needs to be accomplished.

1. **Measurability:**

Objectives need to be measurable so that progress can be tracked effectively. This allows teams to assess whether they are on track or need adjustments.

1. **Relevance:**

Objectives should align with the overall vision and strategy of the organization. They must contribute directly towards its success.

1. **Time-bound:**

Setting deadlines helps create focus and urgency around achieving objectives within a defined timeframe.

Let's take an example of a poorly written objective:

"Increase customer satisfaction."

While this objective seems reasonable at first glance, it lacks the specificity and measurability necessary for effective tracking of progress or outcomes achieved.

Now let's rewrite it using the principles mentioned earlier:

"Increase customer satisfaction scores by 10% within the next quarter through improving response time and implementing personalized support strategies."

This revised objective is specific, measurable, relevant, and time-bound. It clearly outlines the desired outcome, sets a target percentage increase in customer satisfaction scores, and identifies the key actions required to achieve it.

Once objectives are set, organizations can leverage OKRs to measure their progress. OKRs consist of two components: objectives and key results. Objectives define what needs to be achieved, while key results outline specific metrics or milestones that indicate progress toward those objectives.

For instance, let's consider our well-written objective:

Increase customer satisfaction scores by 10% within the next quarter by improving response time and implementing personalized support strategies.

Key Results:

1. Reduce average response time from 24 hours to less than 12 hours.
2. Achieve a minimum Net Promoter Score (NPS) of 8.3. Increase positive customer feedback by 15%.

By setting these key results alongside the objective, teams can monitor their progress objectively and take corrective actions if needed. The use of quantifiable metrics ensures transparency and enables teams to focus on outcomes rather than just outputs.

In addition to measuring progress towards objectives, it is essential to assign business value to features and epics during the planning phase. This helps prioritize work based on its impact on overall organizational goals.

For example:

Feature:

Implement live chat support on our website.

Business Value:

Improve customer experience by providing real-time assistance resulting in increased conversion rates and reduced bounce rates.

By assigning business value upfront, organizations can make informed decisions about which features or epics align closely with their strategic objectives. This ensures that valuable resources are allocated effectively for maximum impact.

Once features are implemented, measuring their actual value becomes crucial in assessing their success or identifying areas for improvement. Metrics such as user engagement, conversion rates, or customer feedback can be used to evaluate the impact of implemented features on the desired objectives.

Writing effective objectives and utilizing OKRs are essential for organizations striving for success. By following the principles of specificity, measurability, relevance, and time-bound nature while crafting objectives, teams can align their efforts toward meaningful goals. The use of OKRs helps measure progress objectively and enables course correction if needed. Assigning business value to features and epics ensures that resources are allocated wisely. Finally, measuring the actual value of implemented features allows organizations to continuously improve and drive toward their desired outcomes.

nineteen

Granularity is a Killer

The Pitfalls of Granularity

As organizations and their teams embrace agility, there often arises a desire to extend this success throughout the entire organization. This hunger for scalability often leads to a heavy emphasis on achieving granular levels of detail. Metrics such as precise capacity planning, expenditure per user story point, and keystrokes per minute by individual team members become the focus.

While these measurements may seem like valuable data to gather, leaders must be cautious in their implementation. Although they may have good intentions, these metrics often result in decreased morale and an excessive amount of time spent on collecting and analyzing data rather than delivering value. The negative outcomes outweigh the benefits of having these additional data points. While some aspects can be automated, it is important to question whether it is truly worth sacrificing the success of agile practices for the sake of gathering "extra" information.

As an agile leader, finding the balance between obtaining more data points and prioritizing customer value delivery is crucial. It is easy to become consumed by demands for greater accountability and understanding from leadership. However, exercising caution is essential.

In pursuit of granular metrics, organizations risk losing sight of their primary goal - delivering high-value products or services to their customers efficiently and effectively. The allure of more precise measurements can overshadow the essence of agility itself - adaptability, collaboration, and responsiveness.

The danger lies in becoming too fixated on numbers that are not inherently aligned with customer needs or business objectives. Agile practices are designed to foster flexibility and responsiveness - qualities that can be hindered by an excessive focus on granular measurements.

Leaders must remember that agility is not about micromanagement or scrutinizing every minute detail but rather about empowering teams to make informed decisions based on broader goals and principles. Instead of drowning in a sea of data points that do not directly contribute to customer satisfaction or business results, leaders should encourage a culture that values continuous improvement through experimentation, feedback loops, and collaboration.

By shifting the focus away from excessive granularity, leaders can redirect their energy toward cultivating an environment that thrives on learning and adaptation. This requires trust in teams' abilities to self-organize, make decisions, and deliver value. Instead of wasting time on perfecting measurements or scrutinizing every keystroke, leaders can support their teams in finding innovative solutions and responding swiftly to changes in the market.

Leaders need to resist the temptation of implementing metrics for the sake of having more data points. Instead, they should prioritize understanding the broader context within which agile practices operate. This includes recognizing that agility is not solely about meeting numerical targets but rather about achieving strategic goals through iterative development, customer feedback, and continuous improvement.

While the desire for granularity may be tempting as organizations strive to scale their agile success further, leaders must exercise caution. The pursuit of excessive data points can lead to decreased morale and a diversion from delivering high-value products or services. Agile leadership requires finding the right balance between obtaining valuable insights and prioritizing customer value delivery. By refocusing efforts on empowering teams and fostering a culture of learning and adaptation, leaders can harness the true essence of agility - delivering results that truly matter to customers while remaining responsive to market changes.

twenty

Task Work vs Knowledge Work

There are two distinct types of work: task work and knowledge work. Understanding the differences between these two types is crucial for leaders who want to embrace agile ways of working. In this chapter, we will explore the characteristics of each type and how they relate to the agile mindset.

Task work is often repetitive and predictable, making it ideal for applying traditional waterfall methods. For centuries, completing projects on time has been considered a measure of success in task-based work. The focus has always been on meeting deadlines and delivering results within a predetermined timeframe. However, when it comes to knowledge work, things take a different turn.

Knowledge work involves activities that require expertise, creativity, and problem-solving skills. Unlike task-based work, it cannot be easily defined by set timelines or repetitive processes. Instead, knowledge work is driven by value creation and building the right things. This fundamental shift in focus requires leaders to rethink their approach to success in an agile environment.

Take this book for example. If I told you there were about 30,000 words in it to read. If you know how many words a minute it takes you to read on average, you could get a pretty good idea of how much time you need to spend on reading it. That's task work.

If I told you to take this book and rewrite several of the chapters, it wouldn't be as easy to estimate or predict when you might finish. One chapter may require much further research than others, there might be some new things to learn to include in the writing, or you might even save time by having AI suggest edits, cutting down on human editors doing that for you. Because this type of work takes thought, discovery and possibly sharing ideas with others first, it's knowledge work.

Completing an effort on time no longer guarantees success in the realm of knowledge work. I once witnessed an Agile Release Train that managed to meet all the deadlines for a new project. The teams were thrilled with their accomplishment, as were their leaders. However, upon closer inspection, it became evident that completing the project on time did not translate into customer satisfaction.

The features that were delivered were not what the customer expected or desired. Despite meeting all deadlines, there was zero value for the customer in what had been accomplished. This example highlights why traditional measures of success do not necessarily apply to agile ways of working in a knowledge-driven environment.

To truly succeed in knowledge work through agility, leaders must shift their perspective on defining success itself. It's no longer about ticking off tasks from a checklist; instead; it's about delivering value as early as possible while adapting to changing requirements along the way.

Agile methodologies thrive in the space of knowledge work precisely because they allow for flexibility, collaboration, and continuous improvement. By embracing an agile mindset, leaders can create an environment that fosters innovation and empowers teams to deliver value in a dynamic and ever-evolving landscape.

To navigate the challenges of knowledge work effectively, leaders must understand its fundamental differences from task work. It requires a shift in thinking from time-based goals to value-based goals. Agile ways of working prioritize delivering the right things over simply meeting deadlines.

By recognizing these distinctions, leaders can approach their teams' work with a fresh perspective. Rather than focusing solely on completing tasks within a set timeframe, they can empower their teams to prioritize value creation and adaptability. This shift in mindset will not only lead to more meaningful outcomes but also increase customer satisfaction and overall project success.

Task work and knowledge work are two distinct types of activities that require different approaches. While task-based work is predictable and lends itself well to traditional project management methods, knowledge-based work is driven by value creation and necessitates an agile mindset.

Leaders who understand the nuances between these two types of work can redefine success in an agile context. By shifting their focus from time-based goals to delivering value as early as possible, they empower their teams to excel at knowledge-driven projects. Embracing agility allows for flexibility, collaboration, and continuous improvement - essential elements for succeeding in today's fast-paced business landscape.

As we delve deeper into the world of agile leadership in the following chapters, we will explore how this shift in perspective impacts team dynamics, decision-making processes, and overall project outcomes. Stay tuned as we uncover the parallels between being an agile leader and being a medical doctor - both requiring adaptability amidst uncertainty while prioritizing patient or customer needs above all else.

twenty-one

When To Chase Waterfalls

Don't go chasing waterfall.

Agile is often hailed as the ultimate solution for all project management woes. However, it is essential to acknowledge that agile methodologies may not always be the most suitable approach. There are instances where waterfall methods prove more effective, particularly when dealing with task-oriented work that is highly predictable and repetitive. In this chapter, we will explore scenarios where chasing waterfalls is indeed the best course of action.

Before delving into specific examples, it is crucial to distinguish between task work and knowledge work. Task work primarily involves routine activities that are systematized and require minimal decision-making. On the other hand, knowledge work encompasses complex problem-solving tasks that demand creativity and adaptability. In this chapter, we will focus on situations where task-oriented work prevails.

1. Manufacturing Processes:

Industries relying on production lines or assembly operations often benefit from a waterfall approach due to their repetitive nature. The sequential progression allows for efficient resource allocation and minimizes disruptions caused by constant changes.

2. Construction Projects:

Large-scale construction projects involve intricate planning, precise scheduling, and tight budget controls. The waterfall methodology ensures a systematic execution of each phase, optimizing resource utilization while maintaining quality standards.

3. Regulatory Compliance:

In industries governed by strict regulatory frameworks such as pharmaceuticals or financial services, a waterfall approach offers clear documentation trails and traceability at each stage of development or implementation.

4. Infrastructure Development:

When building critical infrastructure like highways or bridges, adherence to predefined specifications becomes paramount for safety reasons. By following a waterfall model, project teams can meticulously plan each step while conducting thorough inspections before proceeding further.

5. Legal Procedures:

Legal processes often demand a linear approach due to their inherent structure and reliance on precedence-setting cases or statutes as guidance points throughout the proceedings.

6. Data Migration or System Upgrades:

Complex data migration or system upgrade projects require meticulous planning and rigorous testing. By adopting a waterfall approach, organizations can ensure that each component is thoroughly assessed before moving on to the next phase.

7. Manufacturing Prototypes:

In the initial stages of product development, creating prototypes allows organizations to identify flaws and make necessary adjustments. A waterfall methodology enables a systematic progression from design to production, ensuring stability and minimizing errors.

While waterfall methodologies hold their ground in the aforementioned scenarios, organizations often face situations requiring a blend of agile and waterfall approaches. Implementing a hybrid model allows them to leverage the benefits of both methodologies.

One example of a hybrid approach involves incorporating agile principles during the requirements gathering and design phases while transitioning into a more sequential waterfall process during implementation. This ensures flexibility in adapting to changing customer needs while maintaining structure during execution.

Another hybrid approach could involve breaking down larger projects into smaller components, and applying agile methods for iterative development of those components while using traditional waterfall techniques for overall project management.

Organizations may also adopt an adaptive hybrid model where they choose between agile or waterfall based on specific project constraints or stakeholder preferences. This flexible approach allows them to tailor their project management methodologies according to individual circumstances.

I emphasize that despite agile methodologies' numerous advantages, there are situations where chasing waterfalls is indeed the most sensible choice. Task-oriented work that is repetitive and predictable often thrives under sequential approaches like waterfall. However, organizations must also recognize the value of implementing hybrid models that combine elements from both methodologies for maximum efficiency and adaptability in today's dynamic business environment.

twenty-two

Customer Centricity

Customer centricity has become a vital aspect of success for organizations across industries. The ability to truly understand and meet the needs of customers has proven to be a game-changer in gaining a competitive edge. In this chapter, we will explore what customer centricity entails, the roles individuals play in supporting it, and how it can be effectively implemented throughout an organization.

Customer centricity is not just a buzzword; it represents a fundamental shift in mindset and approach. It is about placing the customer at the heart of every decision and action taken by an organization. Gone are the days when businesses could dictate what customers want or need; instead, they must listen attentively, adapt quickly, and deliver value that aligns with their customers' desires.

To achieve true customer centricity, all members of an organization must rally behind this shared goal. It is not solely the responsibility of product management or marketing teams; rather, it requires cross-functional collaboration and a company-wide commitment to putting customers first.

One essential component of customer centricity is cultivating empathy within teams. By understanding our customers' pain points and challenges on a deep level, we can develop products and services that address these needs effectively. This empathetic approach fosters better relationships with our customers as they feel understood and supported throughout their journey.

Another critical aspect of customer centricity is collecting feedback regularly from our target audience. We must actively seek out their thoughts, opinions, preferences, and suggestions for improvement. This feedback loop allows us to continuously iterate on our offerings based on real-time insights from those who matter most – our customers.

Furthermore, implementing agile methodologies can greatly enhance an organization's ability to embrace customer-centric practices effectively. Agile principles such as iterative development cycles, continuous learning through frequent feedback loops, and empowering self-organizing teams align perfectly with the customer-centric mindset. By embracing agility, organizations can respond swiftly to changing customer needs and deliver value incrementally, ensuring that they remain relevant and ahead of the competition.

To successfully implement customer centricity, organizations should establish clear goals and metrics that align with their customers' outcomes. By measuring success based on how well we meet our customers' needs rather than internal efficiency metrics alone, we can ensure that our efforts are truly focused on delivering value to those we serve.

Leadership plays a crucial role in fostering a customer-centric culture. Agile leaders recognize the importance of empowering their teams and promoting a safe environment for experimentation and innovation. They encourage collaboration across departments and support initiatives that prioritize the voice of the customer.

Customer centricity is no longer optional; it is imperative for any organization seeking long-term success in today's dynamic business landscape. By adopting a mindset where customers are at the forefront of all decision-making processes, organizations can differentiate themselves from the competition and build lasting relationships with their target audience. It requires cross-functional collaboration, empathy-driven approaches, continuous feedback loops, agile methodologies, clear goals aligned with customers' outcomes, and supportive leadership to create a truly customer-centric organization.

In the next chapter, we will dive deeper into how agile leadership principles align with medical practices to further illustrate how being an agile leader is similar to being a medical doctor.

twenty-three

Agile Manifesto Remastered

The Agile Manifesto[1] has been the guiding light for the Agile community for over two decades. While its values and principles have stood the test of time, it is worth considering some enhancements to reflect today's modern ways of working and what we value as important.

Let's begin by examining the values of the Agile Manifesto.

1. Individuals and interactions over processes and tools.

In today's world, where remote work is becoming increasingly common, it is essential to acknowledge the importance of both individuals and their interactions, as well as the tools and processes that enable these interactions to take place. The word "over" can be replaced with "and" to highlight that both individuals and interactions are equally significant. We rely heavily on tools like Zoom and Slack to facilitate effective collaboration, especially when team members are not physically present in the same location.

Suggestion:

Individuals & interactions and processes and tools.

2. Working software over comprehensive documentation.

This value still holds true, but it could benefit from a slight modification. Instead of solely focusing on working software, we should emphasize "Working Software and Valuable Documentation." The reasoning behind this adjustment lies in recognizing that even if a feature is fully developed, without valuable documentation accompanying it, users may struggle to understand or utilize its full potential.

Therefore, valuable documentation should be considered an integral part of delivering a complete product.

Suggestion:

Working Software and Valuable Documentation

3. Customer collaboration over contract negotiation.

This value remains valid; however, there is room for an enhancement that emphasizes customer-centricity throughout all stages of development. Collaboration alone cannot achieve our goals if we do not center our decisions around customer needs.

Therefore, I propose updating this value to read as "Continuous customer centricity over contract negotiation." This adjustment ensures that all aspects of our work revolve around continuously meeting customer expectations.

Suggestion:

Continuous customer centricity over contract negotiation

4. Responding to change over following a plan.

While this value captures the essence of agility in responding to change effectively, it comes across as reactive rather than proactive. To address this, I suggest rephrasing it as "Becoming predictable and expecting change over following a plan."

It is crucial to strive for predictability in our work processes while being prepared for the inevitable changes that come with knowledge work. By anticipating change, we can navigate through uncertainty while maintaining a clear vision of our destination.

Suggestion:

Becoming predictable and expecting change over following a plan

***

AGILE RX: A PRESCRIPTION TO GUIDE AGILE LEADERS

Agile Manifesto Remastered

Individuals & interactions AND processes and tools.

Working Software AND Valuable Documentation

Continuous customer centricity OVER contract negotiation

Becoming predictable & expecting change OVER following a plan

***

In addition to revisiting the values, let's rewrite the **12 principles** of the Agile Manifesto to make them more applicable to any type of work and incorporate modern ways of working.

1. Our highest priority is to satisfy the customer through early and continuous delivery of valuable outcomes.

2. Welcome changing requirements, even late in development. Agile processes harness change for the customer's competitive advantage by adapting swiftly.

3. Deliver valuable tangible results frequently, within shorter timescales ranging from weeks to months, prioritizing shorter iterations.

4. Foster daily collaboration between business people and agile team members throughout the value delivery duration.

5. Build projects around motivated individuals who thrive in an environment that provides necessary support and trust, enabling them to succeed.

6. Face-to-face conversation remains an effective means of conveying information within an agile team; however, virtual communication channels can also be leveraged when necessary.

7. Working outcomes that deliver value are the primary measure of progress across all types of work.

8. Agile processes promote sustainable development by ensuring that sponsors, workers, and users can maintain a consistent pace indefinitely without exhausting resources or compromising quality.

9. Continuous attention to technical excellence and good design enhances agility across various domains of work.

10. Embrace simplicity as an art form - maximize productivity by minimizing unnecessary tasks or complexity wherever possible without sacrificing quality or value delivered.

11. Self-organizing teams foster the emergence of best architectures, requirements, and designs which adapt as needed throughout a value delivery lifecycle regardless of its nature or scale.

12. Regular intervals should be dedicated to team reflection on how to become more effective, allowing for adjustments and fine-tuning of behavior to optimize outcomes.

By enhancing the Agile Manifesto's values and principles, we can ensure that it remains relevant in today's ever-evolving work landscape. These updates capture the essence of agility while accounting for remote work, customer-centricity, predictability, and the diverse range of industries that have embraced agile ways of working.

1 - https://agilemanifesto.org/

twenty-four

Tools of the Trade

Having the right tools at your disposal can make all the difference when it comes to managing product development, value delivery, and continuous improvement. These tools not only help streamline processes but also foster collaboration and ensure efficient project management. In this chapter, we will explore four key types of software tools that Agile leaders can utilize to enhance their effectiveness in leading teams towards success.

1. Agile Project Management Tools:

Agile project management tools serve as a central hub for planning, organizing, and tracking progress on various projects. These tools provide features such as backlog management, sprint planning, task assignment, and progress visualization. One popular example is Jira Software, which allows teams to create user stories or tasks and track them through each stage of development. It provides real-time updates on project status and enables effective communication between team members.

Another notable tool is Trello - a highly visual platform that uses boards and cards to represent tasks or user stories. It allows teams to organize their work in a simple yet powerful way using drag-and-drop functionality. With Trello's integrations with other software applications like Slack or Google Drive, collaboration becomes seamless.

2. Collaboration Tools:

Collaboration lies at the heart of Agile methodologies as it promotes cross-functional teamwork and knowledge sharing among team members. Collaboration tools play a crucial role in facilitating effective communication regardless of geographical barriers.

One such tool is Slack - a messaging platform that enables real-time conversations through channels dedicated to specific topics or projects. It allows instant messaging as well as file sharing within these channels while keeping all team members informed about ongoing discussions.

For document collaboration needs, Google Workspace (formerly G Suite) offers a suite of integrated productivity apps like Google Docs, Sheets, and Slides that allow multiple users to work simultaneously on shared documents from any device with an internet connection.

3. Lean Enterprise and Portfolio Management Tools:

As Agile principles extend beyond individual projects to the management of entire portfolios, Lean Enterprise and Portfolio Management tools come into play. These tools help organizations align their strategic goals with Agile practices, manage budgets, prioritize initiatives, and track overall progress.

A prominent tool in this category is Aha!, which provides a platform for visualizing product roadmaps and strategic plans. It allows Agile leaders to capture customer feedback, define features, prioritize work, and collaborate with various stakeholders throughout the product development lifecycle.

Another notable tool is VersionOne, which offers a comprehensive solution for managing large-scale Agile transformations. It facilitates portfolio planning, program management, and team collaboration while providing real-time visibility into project status and progress.

4. Scaled Agile Tools:

When it comes to scaling Agile methodologies across multiple teams or even entire organizations, specialized tools are necessary to maintain alignment and coordination. These tools enable effective communication between teams working on interdependent projects while ensuring transparency at every level.

One widely used tool in this domain is Atlassian's Jira Align (formerly known as AgileCraft). It provides portfolio-level visibility by aligning strategic initiatives with individual team backlogs. This tool enables leaders to plan epics across multiple teams while maintaining a clear overview of progress through customizable dashboards.

Another valuable tool is from the SAFe (Scaled Agile Framework®), called piplanning.io. This integrates with existing ALM tools like Jira, Azure DevOps, and Rally to offer the ability to do scaled dependency mapping, PI Planning, capacity allocation, and a program board.

Leveraging the right software tools can significantly enhance an Agile leader's ability to manage projects effectively and drive continuous improvement. From project management tools like Jira Software or Trello to collaboration platforms like Slack or Google Workspace - each tool serves a specific purpose in streamlining processes and fostering teamwork.

Additionally, Lean Enterprise and Portfolio Management tools such as Aha! or VersionOne enable strategic alignment at a larger scale, while Scaled Agile tools like Jira Align or SAFe facilitate coordination and transparency when scaling Agile across multiple teams. By embracing these tools, Agile leaders can empower their teams to deliver value faster and with greater efficiency.

twenty-five

Agile Management Tools

Let's take a closer look at some agile project management tools.

These tools are essential for facilitating efficient planning, organization, and tracking of progress in various projects. They serve as a centralized hub that enables teams to effectively manage their work.

In this chapter, we will explore several examples of popular agile management tools and guide you in selecting the most suitable tool for your team.

One widely-used agile management tool is Jira Software. This powerful platform allows teams to create user stories or tasks and track them throughout each stage of development. With its intuitive interface and extensive features, Jira Software provides real-time updates on project status, enabling seamless communication between team members. Its robust backlog management capabilities help prioritize tasks and ensure that the most important work is being addressed first.

Trello is another notable agile management tool that offers a highly visual approach to project management. Using boards and cards to represent tasks or user stories, Trello allows teams to organize their work in a simple yet effective manner. The drag-and-drop functionality makes it easy to move tasks between different stages, providing a visual representation of progress. Furthermore, Trello integrates seamlessly with other software applications such as Slack or Google Drive, fostering collaboration across different platforms.

While Jira Software and Trello are popular choices for agile project management, there are numerous other tools available that cater to different team preferences and requirements.

1. Asana:

Known for its user-friendly interface and comprehensive task-tracking features, Asana offers customizable workflows ideal for managing complex projects.

2. Monday.com:

This versatile tool provides an intuitive platform with customizable templates that can be tailored to fit various project types and team sizes.

3. Basecamp:

With its emphasis on streamlined communication and file-sharing capabilities, Basecamp is an excellent choice for remote teams working on collaborative projects.

4. Wrike:

Suitable for both small-scale teams and large enterprises alike, Wrike offers extensive task management features combined with advanced reporting capabilities.

5. Microsoft Azure DevOps:

Particularly useful for software development projects, this tool offers a range of features including version control, continuous integration, and deployment tracking.

When selecting an agile management tool for your team, it is crucial to consider several factors to ensure the best fit:

1. Team Size and Structure:

Evaluate whether the tool can accommodate the size and structure of your team. Some tools may be better suited for small teams, while others offer scalability for larger organizations.

2. Project Complexity:

Assess whether the tool provides the necessary features to handle your project's complexity. Consider aspects such as task dependencies, resource allocation, and reporting capabilities.

3. Integration Capabilities:

Determine if the tool integrates smoothly with other software applications that your team relies on for collaboration or communication.

4. Ease of Use: Consider the learning curve associated with adopting a new tool. Choose a user-friendly interface that will minimize training time and maximize productivity.

5. Cost: Evaluate the pricing structure of different tools and compare them against your budgetary constraints.

While selecting an agile management tool may seem straightforward, there are common mistakes that many make during this process:

1. Overlooking Team Input:

Failing to involve team members in the decision-making process can lead to resistance or dissatisfaction with the chosen tool.

2. Ignoring Scalability:

Neglecting to consider future growth or changing needs may result in outgrowing a selected tool sooner than anticipated.

3. Overcomplicating Features: Choosing a tool with excessive features that are unnecessary for your team's requirements can lead to confusion and decreased productivity.

4. Disregarding Integration Needs:

Not considering how well a chosen tool integrates with existing systems can hinder effective collaboration between teams using different platforms.

To avoid these mistakes when selecting an agile management tool:

1. Involve key stakeholders from your team in evaluating potential options and gathering feedback on their needs and preferences.

2. Anticipate future growth and select a tool that can scale with your team's expanding requirements.

3. Prioritize simplicity and choose a tool that aligns with your team's specific needs, avoiding unnecessary complexities.

4. Ensure seamless integration by assessing how well the tool integrates with existing software applications that your team relies on.

By carefully considering these factors and avoiding common mistakes, you can select an agile management tool that empowers your team to work more efficiently, collaborate effectively, and successfully deliver projects in an agile environment.

twenty-six

Collaboration Tools

Collaboration lies at the heart of Agile methodologies, as it promotes cross-functional teamwork and knowledge sharing among team members. Effective collaboration is essential for driving innovation and achieving successful project outcomes.

In today's digital age, collaboration tools have become indispensable in facilitating seamless communication and enhancing productivity, regardless of geographical barriers.

One such tool that has gained popularity among Agile teams is Slack. Slack is a messaging platform that enables real-time conversations through channels dedicated to specific topics or projects. It allows team members to engage in instant messaging and file sharing within these channels, ensuring that everyone stays informed about ongoing discussions. With its user-friendly interface and robust features, Slack has become a go-to tool for Agile teams looking to foster effective communication.

Another valuable tool for document collaboration needs is Google Workspace (formerly known as G Suite). This suite of integrated productivity apps includes Google Docs, Sheets, and Slides, which allow multiple users to work simultaneously on shared documents from any device with an internet connection. This feature greatly enhances the efficiency of collaborative work by eliminating the need for version control issues and enabling real-time updates.

While Slack and Google Workspace are excellent options for facilitating collaboration within Agile teams, there are several other tools available in the market that can cater to different needs. When selecting a collaboration tool, it is important to consider certain key factors:

AGILE RX: A PRESCRIPTION TO GUIDE AGILE LEADERS

1. Ease of use: The selected tool should have a user-friendly interface that requires minimal training or technical expertise. A complicated or unintuitive tool can hinder adoption within the team.

2. Integration capabilities: The chosen tool should seamlessly integrate with other commonly used software applications within the organization, such as project management tools or customer relationship management systems.

3. Communication features: Look for features like instant messaging, video conferencing capabilities, and virtual meeting rooms to facilitate effective communication among team members.

4. File sharing capabilities: Ensure that the tool allows easy file sharing between team members, with the ability to track changes and maintain version control.

5. Security and privacy: Data security is paramount when collaborating on sensitive projects. Choose a tool that offers robust security measures, such as encryption and access controls, to safeguard confidential information.

6. Mobile accessibility: In today's mobile-driven world, it is essential for collaboration tools to have mobile apps or responsive web interfaces that allow team members to stay connected and contribute on the go.

7. Scalability: Consider the scalability of the tool, especially if your team is expected to grow in size or if you anticipate working on larger projects in the future. The tool should be able to accommodate increasing collaboration needs without compromising performance.

8. Cost-effectiveness: Evaluate the pricing structure of different collaboration tools and choose one that aligns with your budget while offering the necessary features and functionality required by your team.

By carefully considering these factors when selecting a collaboration tool, Agile leaders can ensure they choose a solution that best suits their team's needs and enhances their ability to collaborate effectively.

Collaboration tools are invaluable assets for Agile teams seeking seamless communication and enhanced productivity. Slack and Google Workspace are popular choices due to their user-friendly interfaces and comprehensive features. However, Agile leaders need to evaluate other options based on factors such as ease of use, integration capabilities, communication features, file-sharing capabilities, security measures, mobile accessibility, scalability potential, and cost-effectiveness.

By selecting the right collaboration tool(s), Agile leaders can empower their teams with efficient means of communication and foster a collaborative environment conducive to success.

twenty-seven

Prescriptions - Agile Frameworks

Prescribing a framework is akin to prescribing medicine. Much like different medicines address different ailments and sicknesses, various Agile frameworks exist to solve different situations. However, just as one medicine may work for one person but not for another with the same illness, one framework may help some teams or organizations while falling short for others.

The key reason behind this discrepancy lies in the fact that many Agile leaders and coaches fail to delve into the root cause of the problem at hand. Similar to doctors who merely treat symptoms without investigating their underlying cause, these individuals often miss out on identifying and addressing the true source of challenges within an organization.

To truly discover the root cause of the biggest problems and challenges faced by an organization, it is imperative to adopt a systematic approach. Here are some suggestions on how to effectively uncover these underlying issues:

1. Conduct thorough analysis:

Start by conducting comprehensive analyses of your organization's structure, processes, and culture. This involves closely examining how teams interact, identifying communication gaps or bottlenecks, evaluating decision-making processes, and assessing overall employee engagement levels. By gaining a deep understanding of these aspects, you can pinpoint areas where improvement is needed.

2. Engage with stakeholders:

To gain valuable insights into organizational challenges, engage directly with key stakeholders such as team members at all levels, managers, executives, and even customers or clients if applicable. Ask open-ended questions about their experiences working within the current Agile framework or any pain points they have identified along the way. Encourage honest feedback and ensure anonymity if necessary to foster transparency.

3. Utilize data-driven approaches:

Leverage data analytics tools and techniques to analyze quantitative data related to project progress, team performance metrics (e.g., velocity), customer satisfaction scores, or feedback from retrospective meetings. This will provide concrete evidence regarding areas that need improvement or potential pain points affecting teams' productivity and effectiveness.

4. Employ root cause analysis techniques:

Adopt proven root cause analysis techniques, such as the "5 Whys" method or Ishikawa diagrams, to dig deeper into the underlying causes of specific problems. By repeatedly asking "why" until arriving at the fundamental reason behind an issue, you can uncover systemic issues that may not be immediately evident.

5. Encourage a culture of continuous improvement:

Create an environment where teams are encouraged to continuously improve their processes and address challenges openly. Foster a culture that values learning from failures and treats them as opportunities for growth rather than sources of blame. By promoting open dialogue, collaboration, and experimentation, you can encourage individuals to surface underlying problems and propose innovative solutions.

6. Seek external expertise:

Consider engaging external consultants or experts in Agile practices who can provide fresh perspectives and insights based on their experiences working with various organizations. These professionals bring a wealth of knowledge about different Agile frameworks and can help identify which one might be most suitable for your organization's unique challenges.

Remember that discovering the root cause is just the first step in solving organizational problems effectively. Once you have uncovered these underlying issues, it is crucial to select an appropriate Agile framework that aligns with your organization's specific needs.

In the following chapters, we will delve into some of the most widely used Agile frameworks in more detail, exploring their strengths, weaknesses, and situations where they excel. By understanding these frameworks thoroughly and considering them within the context of your organization's unique challenges, you will be better equipped to prescribe the right framework - just like a doctor prescribing medicine tailored to an individual patient's needs.

In summary, agile leaders must take care not to rush into prescribing agile frameworks without first understanding the root causes of organizational challenges. By following systematic approaches such as comprehensive analysis, stakeholder engagement, data-driven methods, root cause analysis techniques, fostering a culture of continuous improvement, and seeking external expertise when necessary, leaders can gain valuable insights that will inform their choice of an appropriate agile framework. In doing so, they can effectively address the specific needs of their organization and guide teams towards greater success in their Agile journey.

twenty-eight

Frameworks - Scrum

In the previous chapters, we explored various facets of Agile leadership and how it parallels the role of a medical doctor. We delved into the importance of empathy, adaptability, and continuous learning. Now, let us turn our attention to one of the most widely used frameworks in Agile methodology: Scrum.

Scrum is often associated with software development teams, but its principles can be applied to any project or organization seeking to embrace agility. In this chapter, we will discuss how Agile leaders can support their teams and the organization by utilizing the Scrum framework.

The Scrum framework revolves around small cross-functional teams that work collaboratively towards a common goal within short time increments called sprints. These sprints typically last two to four weeks and enable teams to deliver valuable increments of work at regular intervals. As an Agile leader, your role is crucial in ensuring that your team effectively utilizes Scrum principles.

One primary responsibility of an Agile leader when implementing Scrum is creating a supportive environment for their team members. This involves fostering open communication channels, encouraging transparency, and promoting trust within the team. By doing so, you empower your team members to voice their opinions freely and contribute actively during sprint planning sessions or daily stand-ups.

As an Agile leader using the Scrum framework, it is essential to understand that your role transforms from being a traditional manager into a servant leader. Rather than dictating tasks or micromanaging your team's activities, you act as a facilitator who supports their needs and removes any impediments they may encounter along their journey.

Furthermore, being an effective servant-leader means empowering your team by providing them with autonomy over their work while ensuring alignment with organizational goals. This autonomy allows them to make decisions independently while still being accountable for delivering value within each sprint cycle.

Another critical aspect for Agile leaders utilizing Scrum is embracing continuous improvement practices. The retrospective, a key ceremony in Scrum, provides an opportunity for your team to reflect on their work and identify areas for improvement. As an Agile leader, you play a vital role in facilitating these retrospectives and guiding your team towards actionable insights.

During retrospectives, encourage your team members to share their observations openly and honestly. Create a safe space where they can discuss both successes and challenges encountered during the sprint. By fostering a culture of continuous learning and improvement, you enable your team to adapt their processes effectively and enhance their performance over time.

While Scrum is often associated with software development teams, its principles can be applied beyond this context. Agile leaders can explore how the Scrum framework could benefit other departments or projects within the organization.

For instance, consider implementing Scrum principles in marketing campaigns or product launches. By breaking down complex tasks into smaller increments and establishing short feedback loops with stakeholders, teams can quickly respond to changing market dynamics and deliver valuable outcomes more frequently.

As an Agile leader utilizing the Scrum framework, your role is crucial in creating a supportive environment for your team members while embracing servant-leadership practices. By empowering your team through autonomy and continuous improvement, you enable them to deliver value consistently within each sprint cycle.

Remember that Scrum's principles are not limited to software development teams only. Explore how these principles could benefit other areas of the organization by fostering collaboration, transparency, and adaptability throughout various projects.

By embracing the mindset of an Agile leader and leveraging the power of Scrum's framework appropriately tailored to suit different contexts within your organization, you will pave the way for success in achieving agility at both individual and organizational levels.

twenty-nine

Frameworks - Kanban

Empowering Lean Agile Leaders

In the ever-evolving landscape of Agile leadership, leaders must equip themselves with versatile frameworks that can support their teams and organizations. One such framework that has gained significant popularity is Kanban. Originally developed in the manufacturing industry, Kanban has found its way into various domains, including software development. This chapter explores how Agile leaders can leverage the power of Kanban to drive efficiency, transparency, and continuous improvement within their teams.

Understanding Kanban:

Kanban, at its core, is a visual framework designed to manage work effectively by visualizing the workflow and promoting a steady flow of tasks. It provides real-time visibility into work items as they progress through different stages of completion, enabling teams to identify bottlenecks and streamline their processes.

Applying Kanban in Software Development:

Agile leaders have discovered that Kanban can be seamlessly integrated into software development practices to enhance collaboration and productivity. By utilizing a Kanban board – typically consisting of columns representing different stages like "To Do," "In Progress," and "Done" – teams gain a shared understanding of work status and dependencies.

The beauty of adopting Kanban lies in its simplicity. Unlike other methodologies with predefined iterations or time-bound sprints, Kanban embraces a more flexible approach by allowing teams to pull new work only when they have capacity. This empowers individuals within the team to focus on delivering value incrementally while minimizing context switching.

Benefits Beyond Software Teams:

While initially conceived for manufacturing processes and later adapted for software development, Agile leaders are finding innovative ways to extend the benefits of Kanban beyond these realms. Several other areas within organizations can embrace this framework's principles to optimize their workflows.

For instance:

1. Marketing teams can utilize a Kanban board to manage campaigns from ideation through execution phases.
2. Human Resources departments can employ a similar approach for managing recruitment processes, from initial screening to onboarding.
3. Customer support teams can visualize customer queries and track their resolution progress using a Kanban board, ensuring timely responses and efficient service delivery.

Kanban's Impact on Agile Leadership:

Agile leaders embracing Kanban witness a paradigm shift in their leadership style. The framework encourages transparency, autonomy, and collaboration while fostering a culture of continuous improvement.

By visualizing work items on a Kanban board, leaders gain real-time insights into team capacity and workload distribution. This visibility enables them to identify overburdened team members or bottlenecks in the workflow promptly. Armed with this knowledge, Agile leaders can make informed decisions regarding resource allocation and process improvements.

Moreover, Kanban promotes self-organization within teams. Rather than micromanaging individuals' tasks, Agile leaders empower their team members to take ownership of their work and prioritize effectively. This autonomy instills a sense of accountability and fosters creativity among team members.

Continuous improvement is at the core of Agile methodologies, and Kanban complements this philosophy seamlessly. By encouraging teams to reflect regularly on their processes using techniques like retrospective meetings, leaders can drive incremental enhancements that lead to higher efficiency, reduced waste, and increased customer satisfaction.

Conclusion:

In the journey towards becoming an Agile leader who drives transformational change within organizations, embracing frameworks like Kanban is essential. Its principles enable teams to visualize work progress transparently while promoting autonomy and collaboration. From software development to various other domains within organizations, the versatility of Kanban empowers leaders to facilitate continuous improvement for better outcomes.

As an Agile leader leveraging the power of Kanban in your daily practices, you unlock the potential for your teams to thrive in an environment that values flexibility, efficiency, and innovation. Embrace this framework with open arms as you embark upon your quest for excellence in leadership – let it be your guiding light towards becoming an empowered Agile leader who leads by example!

thirty

Frameworks - Scaled Agile Framework (SAFe)®

As we delve deeper into the world of Agile leadership, it is crucial to understand the various frameworks that can be employed to guide an organization's Agile transformation. One such framework that has gained significant popularity in recent years is the Scaled Agile Framework[1], commonly known as SAFe. SAFe represents a combination of Scrum, Kanban, and XP methodologies, all underpinned by Lean-Agile principles.

To truly comprehend when it makes sense for an organization to utilize SAFe, we must first grasp what this framework entails. At its core, SAFe provides a structured approach to scaling Agile practices across large enterprises. It addresses the challenges faced when multiple teams need to collaborate effectively while maintaining alignment with business objectives. By incorporating elements from Scrum, Kanban, and XP methodologies into a cohesive system, SAFe offers organizations a roadmap for achieving agility at scale.

However, despite its numerous benefits and well-defined structure, many organizations fail to fully reap the rewards of implementing SAFe. One common pitfall lies in attempting to follow the framework rigidly without considering their unique context or specific needs. While SAFe provides valuable guidelines and best practices for scaling Agile practices effectively, it is vital to remember that it is just that - a framework. It should serve as a starting point rather than a set of rules etched in stone.

Agile leaders play a pivotal role in supporting the successful utilization of SAFe within their organizations. They act as catalysts for change by fostering an environment where experimentation and continuous improvement are encouraged. An Agile leader understands that while adhering strictly to every aspect of SAFe might not be feasible or appropriate for every organization or team, aligning their actions with core Lean-Agile principles can lead them on the path towards agility.

One key aspect that distinguishes an effective implementation of SAFe from an unsuccessful one lies in the ability to adapt the framework to fit the organization's unique circumstances. This flexibility allows organizations to tailor SAFe to their specific needs and make adjustments as they progress on their Agile journey. By understanding that SAFe is not a one-size-fits-all solution, Agile leaders can leverage its principles and adapt them accordingly, while keeping their organization's goals and context in mind.

While SAFe may be a popular choice for scaling Agile practices, it is essential to acknowledge that it is not the only option available. Depending on an organization's size, industry, or culture, alternative frameworks might be better suited to achieve agility at scale. For instance, organizations with more fluid requirements or those operating in highly innovative industries may find frameworks like LeSS (Large-Scale Scrum) or Nexus more suitable.

SAFe serves as a powerful framework for scaling Agile practices across large enterprises. However, organizations must approach its implementation with caution and recognize that it should be adapted to fit their unique context rather than blindly adhering to every aspect of the framework. Agile leaders play a crucial role in supporting the successful adoption of SAFe by aligning actions with Lean-Agile principles and fostering a culture of continuous improvement. Finally, organizations need to consider alternative frameworks when they better align with their specific needs and goals.

By fully understanding when and how to utilize SAFe effectively while also considering alternative frameworks when appropriate, Agile leaders can navigate the complexities of scaling Agile practices successfully within their organizations. Only then can they truly harness the power of agility at scale and propel their teams toward unprecedented levels of collaboration, innovation, and ultimately success.

1 - https://scaledagileframework.com/

thirty-one

Frameworks - FAST Agile

As an Agile leader, it is crucial to have a clear understanding of various Agile frameworks and methodologies to effectively guide your team. One such framework that has gained popularity in recent years is the FAST Agile framework.

In this chapter, we will explore what the FAST Agile framework entails, who created it, why it might be needed, and how Agile leaders can implement it successfully.

The FAST Agile framework was developed by Ron Quartel[1] to address some common challenges faced by organizations implementing Agile practices. It stands for Flow, Alignment, Stability, and Transparency - four key pillars that form the foundation of this framework.

Flow:

At its core, the Flow principle aims to ensure a smooth and uninterrupted flow of work within an organization. This involves eliminating bottlenecks and reducing waste to achieve efficient delivery. By focusing on flow optimization, teams can minimize interruptions and improve overall productivity.

Alignment:

Alignment refers to the synchronization of goals and objectives across teams within an organization. It emphasizes the importance of shared purpose and collaboration towards achieving common goals. With proper alignment, teams can work together seamlessly toward delivering value to customers.

Stability:

Stability emphasizes creating a stable environment where teams can thrive. This involves providing a sense of security through consistent processes, reliable tools, and supportive leadership. By fostering stability within an organization, teams are more likely to perform at their best without unnecessary distractions or disruptions.

Transparency:

Transparency plays a vital role in building trust among team members and stakeholders alike. It involves open communication channels where information flows freely without barriers or hidden agendas. With transparency as a guiding principle, organizations can encourage collaboration while minimizing misunderstandings or misinterpretations.

Implementing the FAST Agile framework requires careful consideration from Agile leaders. Here are some steps they can take:

1. Educate Yourself: As an agile leader interested in implementing the FAST Agile framework effectively within your organization, it is crucial to gain a thorough understanding of its principles and concepts. Read up on the framework, attend training sessions, and seek guidance from experts in the field to ensure you are well-equipped for the journey ahead.

2. Assess Current State: Before implementing any new framework, it is essential to assess your organization's current state. Evaluate existing Agile practices, identify areas of improvement, and determine how the FAST Agile framework aligns with your organization's goals and objectives.

3. Plan for Change: Implementing a new framework often requires change management strategies. Develop a comprehensive plan that outlines the steps involved in implementing the FAST Agile framework, including communication strategies, training programs, and support mechanisms for your teams.

4. Foster Collaboration: The FAST Agile framework emphasizes collaboration as a key element of success. Encourage cross-functional teams to work together closely, promote knowledge sharing, and

create an environment where everyone feels comfortable contributing their ideas.

5. Monitor Progress: Regularly track and monitor progress throughout the implementation process. Use metrics such as lead time, cycle time, or customer satisfaction to measure improvements resulting from adopting the FAST Agile framework.

6. Adapt and Evolve: The Agile landscape is continuously evolving; hence it is essential to stay adaptable as an agile leader. Keep learning about emerging trends and best practices within Agile methodologies to ensure you can adapt the FAST Agile framework as needed within your organization.

By embracing the principles of Flow, Alignment, Stability, and Transparency offered by the FAST Agile framework, agile leaders can guide their organizations toward improved efficiency and collaboration while delivering value consistently.

Understanding different frameworks such as FAST Agile is crucial for agile leaders seeking continuous improvement within their organizations' delivery processes. By implementing this powerful framework effectively while focusing on flow optimization, alignment of goals across teams ensures stability in processes while promoting transparency throughout all levels of operation - agility will become inherent in every facet of an organization's operations.

1 - https://www.fast-agile.com/contact

thirty-two

Frameworks - LeSS

LeSS is More

There are various frameworks available to help organizations scale their agile practices. One such framework is LeSS[1], which stands for Large-Scale Scrum. In this chapter, we will explore what the LeSS framework entails, its advantages and disadvantages compared to other scaling agile frameworks, and how Agile leaders can effectively utilize this framework to lead their organization toward better ways of working.

Understanding LeSS:

LeSS is a lightweight framework that focuses on scaling Scrum principles and practices to large organizations. It emphasizes simplicity, transparency, and empirical process control. Unlike some other scaling frameworks that introduce additional roles and complexities, LeSS promotes keeping things simple by relying on basic Scrum principles.

Advantages of LeSS:

One significant advantage of using the LeSS framework is its simplicity. By adhering closely to core Scrum principles without introducing unnecessary complexity or additional roles, teams can focus on delivering value rather than being burdened by excessive processes or hierarchy.

Another advantage is the emphasis on transparency throughout the organization. The LeSS framework encourages open communication channels and visibility into work progress at all levels. This helps teams collaborate more effectively, identify bottlenecks or issues early on, and make necessary adjustments promptly.

Additionally, by scaling down traditional organizational structures into smaller self-organizing teams within a broader context, LeSS enables faster decision-making processes. This agility allows organizations to respond swiftly to changing market demands or customer needs.

Disadvantages of LeSS:

While there are numerous benefits to using the LeSS framework, it's essential to recognize that it may not be suitable for every organization. One potential disadvantage lies in its simplicity; some organizations with complex structures or diverse product portfolios may find it challenging to adapt without additional customizations or extensions.

Furthermore, implementing the LeSS framework requires a cultural shift within an organization towards self-organization and decentralized decision-making. This can be a significant challenge for organizations accustomed to traditional hierarchical structures, where decision-making is centralized.

Tools Supporting LeSS:

Several tools support the effective implementation of the LeSS framework. One such tool is LeSS Canvas, which provides a visual representation of the various components involved in scaling Scrum, such as product definition, organizational design, and feature teams. The canvas helps Agile leaders gain an overview of their organization's current state and identify areas for improvement.

Another tool commonly used in conjunction with LeSS is the LeSS Sprint Review Tool. This tool enables distributed teams to collaborate effectively during sprint reviews by providing a virtual space for sharing progress updates, gathering feedback, and making decisions collectively.

Additionally, Agile leaders can leverage various project management software or agile collaboration platforms that offer features tailored to scaling agile practices. These tools often include functionalities like backlog management, sprint planning boards, real-time communication channels, and progress-tracking dashboards.

Conclusion:

The LeSS framework offers a straightforward yet powerful approach to scaling Scrum principles within large organizations. Its focus on simplicity and transparency fosters collaboration and empowers self-organizing teams to deliver value more efficiently. However, Agile leaders must assess whether the framework aligns with their organization's specific needs before embarking on its implementation journey.

By utilizing supporting tools like LeSS Canvas and embracing agile project management software or collaboration platforms tailored for scaling agile practices, Agile leaders can navigate the challenges associated with implementing the LeSS framework successfully.

In the previous chapter, we explored another popular scaling agile framework - SAFe (Scaled Agile Framework) - highlighting its distinctive characteristics compared to LeSS and providing insights into how Agile leaders can leverage SAFe effectively in their organizations. In the next chapter, we will dive into SaS or Scrum at Scale.

1 - https://less.works/less/framework

thirty-three

Frameworks - Scrum at Scale (SaS)

In the previous chapters, we have explored various Agile frameworks and methodologies such as Scrum, Kanban, Lean, and other scaling frameworks. These frameworks have been instrumental in helping organizations embrace agility and deliver value to their customers. However, as organizations grow and become more complex, a need arises for scaling Agile practices to ensure seamless collaboration across multiple teams.

In this chapter, we will delve into the Scrum at Scale (SaS)[1] framework – its creation, purpose, implementation strategies for Agile Leaders, and an analysis of its advantages and limitations.

The Birth of Scrum at Scale:

Scrum at Scale is the brainchild of Dr. Jeff Sutherland and Alex Brown. It was developed to address the challenges faced by large organizations when implementing Scrum across multiple teams. Driven by their passion for agility and continuous improvement, they embarked on creating a framework that could scale the benefits of Scrum while maintaining its core principles.

The Purpose of SaS:

Scrum at Scale aims to enable organizations to scale their Agile practices effectively without sacrificing flexibility or responsiveness. By creating a structure that maintains alignment and coordination among numerous teams working towards a common goal, SaS empowers enterprises to adapt swiftly in today's fast-paced business environment.

Implementation Strategies for Agile Leaders:

As an Agile Leader embracing the role of an "Agile Doctor," it is crucial to understand how SaS can be implemented within your organization:

1. Establishing a Product Owner Team: Create a Product Owner team composed of representatives from each team involved in delivering value. This team will collaborate closely with stakeholders to define clear product goals and prioritize work accordingly.

2. Building a Meta-Scrum: The Meta-Scrum serves as the coordinating body for all teams involved in delivering products or services. As an Agile Leader, you should facilitate regular Meta-Scrum meetings where representatives from each team come together to discuss progress, dependencies, and impediments.

3. Coordinating Backlog Refinement: Encourage Product Owners and Scrum Masters to collaborate on backlog refinement sessions. This ensures that dependencies are identified early on, and the backlog is continuously groomed to maintain a steady flow of work across teams.

4. Implementing the Scrum of Scrums: The Scrum of Scrums is a critical component of SaS, enabling coordination among multiple teams. Agile Leaders should facilitate regular Scrum of Scrums meetings where representatives from each team share updates, address cross-team dependencies, and align their efforts toward achieving the organization's goals.

Advantages of SaS:

Scrum at Scale offers several benefits for organizations looking to scale Agile practices:

1. Enhanced Collaboration: SaS fosters collaboration across teams by providing a structured framework for communication and coordination. This leads to increased efficiency and smoother integration between various parts of an organization.

2. Improved Alignment: By establishing clear product goals through the Product Owner team and Meta-Scrum meetings, SaS ensures alignment among all teams involved in delivering value. This alignment helps avoid duplication of efforts while maximizing business outcomes.

3. Flexibility without Sacrificing Consistency: SaS allows for flexibility

at both the team level and organizational level while maintaining consistency in terms of core principles and values. It enables teams to adapt their processes as needed without compromising the overall integrity of Agile practices.

Limitations and Considerations:

While Scrum at Scale provides an effective approach for scaling Agile practices, it is essential to acknowledge its limitations:

1. Learning Curve: Implementing SaS requires understanding its intricacies and adapting existing processes accordingly. Agile Leaders need to invest time in learning about the framework before introducing it within their organizations.
2. Cultural Change: Scaling Agile practices involves a cultural shift within an organization. Resistance to change may arise from individuals who are accustomed to traditional hierarchical structures or siloed ways of working. Agile Leaders should be prepared to address these challenges and foster a culture of agility.

Conclusion:

Scrum at Scale (SaS) offers a powerful framework for scaling Agile practices within organizations. By embracing SaS, Agile Leaders can establish effective coordination mechanisms, enhance collaboration, and ensure alignment across multiple teams. While the implementation of SaS may require effort and cultural change, its benefits in terms of improved efficiency and adaptability make it a valuable tool for organizations aiming to thrive in today's dynamic business landscape. As an Agile Leader, your role is akin to that of a medical doctor – diagnosing organizational ailments, prescribing agile remedies, and guiding the transformation towards agility with frameworks like Scrum at Scale.

1 - https://www.scrumatscale.com/

thirty-four

Frameworks - Nexus

In the previous chapter, we explored Scrum at Scale. Each framework we highlighted so far has its unique advantages and challenges. In this chapter, we will delve into the Nexus^{TM} framework and understand how Agile leaders can leverage it to achieve their scaling agility goals.

Nexus^{TM} is another scaled Scrum framework designed specifically for large-scale software development projects. It provides a structure that enables multiple Scrum teams to work together cohesively towards a common goal. The primary objective of Nexus^{TM} is to enhance communication and collaboration among teams while ensuring consistent and timely delivery of valuable software increments.

One of the key components of Nexus^{TM} is the Nexus Integration Team (NIT). The NIT consists of representatives from each Scrum team involved in the project. Their role is to coordinate dependencies, resolve inter-team issues, and maintain alignment across all teams. By having dedicated individuals solely focused on integration, organizations can minimize delays caused by dependencies and improve overall productivity.

Implementing Nexus^{TM} brings several benefits to organizations striving for agility at scale. Firstly, it fosters transparency by providing visibility into each team's progress through regular Nexus^{TM} events such as the Daily Nexus Scrum, Sprint Planning Nexus, and Sprint Review Nexus. This transparency helps identify bottlenecks early on and facilitates continuous improvement.

Secondly, Nexus^{TM} promotes collaboration among teams by emphasizing cross-team coordination through its NIT structure. By breaking down silos and encouraging open communication channels between teams, knowledge sharing becomes natural, leading to improved efficiency and reduced rework.

Thirdly, as with any scaled framework, Nexus^{TM} helps organizations address complexity by providing a defined structure that guides them in scaling their agile practices effectively. It offers clear roles and responsibilities within each team while establishing guidelines for inter-team interactions.

However, like any other framework or methodology, there are also some challenges associated with implementing Nexus^{TM}. One major challenge lies in maintaining synchronization between multiple teams working on different parts of the product. It requires constant communication and coordination to ensure that all teams are aligned and progressing towards the same goal.

Another challenge is the potential for increased overhead due to additional Nexus^{TM}-specific events and artifacts. While these events and artifacts serve a purpose in facilitating coordination, they can also add extra administrative burden if not managed efficiently.

To support the successful implementation of Nexus^{TM}, Agile leaders play a crucial role. They need to provide guidance, support, and advocacy for the adoption of Nexus^{TM} within their organizations. Here are some key actions Agile leaders can take:

1. Educate and train: Agile leaders should ensure that all team members understand the principles behind Nexus^{TM} and how it fits into the overall agility journey. Providing training sessions or workshops on Nexus^{TM} can help teams grasp its concepts more effectively.
2. Facilitate collaboration: Agile leaders should foster an environment that encourages collaboration between teams by promoting cross-team knowledge-sharing sessions, setting up regular meetings between Scrum Masters, or facilitating joint retrospectives.
3. Remove impediments: Agile leaders need to identify and remove any obstacles that hinder the effective implementation of Nexus^{TM}. This

may involve addressing organizational resistance to change or resolving conflicts between teams.

4. Monitor progress: Agile leaders should keep a close eye on the progress of each team within Nexus^{TM} by attending Nexus^{TM} events, gathering feedback from team members, and monitoring key metrics such as velocity or cycle time. This allows them to identify areas for improvement proactively.

5. Celebrate successes: Recognizing achievements is crucial in maintaining motivation and momentum within teams working under Nexus^{TM}. Agile leaders should celebrate milestones reached or valuable contributions made by individuals or teams involved in scaling agility with Nexus^{TM}.

Implementing the Nexus^{TM} framework can be instrumental in scaling agility within organizations undertaking large-scale software development projects. By promoting transparency, and collaboration, and providing a structured approach to scaling agile practices, organizations can overcome complexity while maintaining alignment across multiple teams.

Agile leaders play a vital role in supporting the successful implementation of Nexus^{TM}. Through education, facilitation, impediment removal, progress monitoring, and celebration of successes, they can guide their teams toward achieving their scaling agility goals. With Nexus^{TM} as a backbone, organizations can navigate the challenges of scaling agility and deliver valuable software increments consistently.

1 - https://www.scrum.org/resources/nexus-guide

thirty-five

Frameworks - Disciplined Agile (DA)

T*he Artist Formerly Known As Disciplined Agile Delivery (DAD)*[1]

In the ever-evolving landscape of Agile methodologies, frameworks play a crucial role in guiding organizations toward successful implementation and scaling. One such framework that has transformed is Disciplined Agile (DA), formerly known as Disciplined Agile Delivery (DAD). This chapter explores the reasons behind this name change and delves into how Agile leaders can leverage the power of DA to achieve their scaling agile goals.

1. The Evolution of Disciplined Agile

As with any framework, Disciplined Agile has evolved to better align with industry needs and best practices. Originally introduced as Disciplined Agile Delivery, it focused primarily on delivery teams and guided how to bring discipline into the agile process. However, as organizations began to embrace agility at an enterprise level, there arose a need for a more comprehensive framework that could scale across teams and departments.

To address this demand, the creators of DA recognized that agility goes beyond just delivery; it encompasses all aspects of an organization's operations. With this realization, they expanded the scope of the framework and rebranded it as Disciplined Agile. This new name reflects its broader applicability across various business functions, emphasizing its ability to foster agility throughout an entire organization.

2. Implementing Disciplined Agile for Scaling Agility

Agile leaders face unique challenges when it comes to scaling agility within their organizations. They must strike a delicate balance between empowering autonomous teams and ensuring alignment towards common goals.

Disciplined Agile provides them with a roadmap for achieving this balance by offering a flexible yet structured approach.

One key aspect of implementing DA is embracing its principle of choice-driven agility. Unlike rigid methodologies that prescribe specific practices or processes, DA enables teams to tailor their approach based on contextual factors such as team size, domain complexity, organizational culture, and regulatory requirements. This flexibility allows Agile leaders to adapt and fine-tune their implementation, ensuring that it aligns with the unique needs of their organization.

Another critical element of DA is its focus on continuous improvement. Agile leaders must foster a culture of learning and experimentation within their teams. The framework encourages regular retrospectives, where teams reflect on their practices, identify areas for improvement, and take action to address them. By embracing this iterative approach, organizations can continuously evolve and optimize their agile processes.

Additionally, Disciplined Agile emphasizes the importance of collaboration across teams and departments. It guides how to establish effective cross-functional collaborations, enabling seamless coordination between different parts of the organization. This collaborative mindset fosters knowledge sharing, and innovation, and ultimately drives organizational agility.

3. Overcoming Challenges with Disciplined Agile

Implementing any framework comes with its own set of challenges, and Disciplined Agile is no exception. One common hurdle is resistance from team members who may be accustomed to traditional ways of working or are skeptical about agile methodologies altogether. Agile leaders must address these concerns by providing education and training around the benefits of DA while emphasizing its adaptability to suit different contexts.

Another challenge lies in maintaining consistency across multiple teams when scaling agility at an enterprise level. Disciplined Agile offers guidance on how to establish governance structures that provide oversight without stifling autonomy. This ensures that teams have the necessary support while still retaining the flexibility required for agile practices.ConclusionDisciplined Agile holds immense potential for organizations seeking to scale agility beyond individual teams or projects. By embracing this framework's principles of choice-driven agility, continuous improvement, and collaboration, Agile leaders can steer their organizations toward success in an increasingly complex business landscape.

The transformation from Disciplined Agile Delivery (DAD) to Disciplined Agile (DA) signifies a broader perspective on organizational agility – one that recognizes the need for flexibility in all aspects beyond just delivery processes. As an Agile leader, understanding and implementing the principles of DA can unlock new avenues for growth, efficiency, and adaptability within your organization.

1 - https://www.pmi.org/disciplined-agile/introduction-to-disciplined-agile

thirty-six

Frameworks - Enterprise Kanban or Portfolio Kanban

Another scaling framework that has gained significant recognition is Enterprise Kanban. In this chapter, we will explore the benefits and drawbacks of using this framework and how Agile Leaders can effectively implement and leverage it to accomplish their goals.

Enterprise Kanban, a variant of the popular Kanban method, offers a systematic approach to managing work at an organizational level. It provides a visual representation of workflow, promotes collaboration across teams, and fosters continuous improvement. By utilizing Enterprise Kanban, Agile Leaders can streamline processes, enhance transparency, and optimize resource allocation.

One of the key advantages of Enterprise Kanban is its flexibility. Unlike traditional project management methodologies that rely on fixed schedules and detailed planning upfront, this framework allows for adaptability in response to changing circumstances. Agile Leaders can easily reallocate resources or adjust priorities based on evolving business needs without disrupting ongoing work. This dynamic nature enables organizations to stay responsive in a rapidly changing market landscape.

Another benefit lies in Enterprise Kanban's ability to promote transparency throughout the organization. With its visual boards displaying work items at various stages of completion, everyone has visibility into ongoing projects and their current status. This increased transparency fosters a culture of accountability as team members take ownership of their tasks and collaborate more effectively across departments.

Furthermore, using Enterprise Kanban encourages continuous improvement within teams and organizations as a whole. By visualizing workflow bottlenecks or inefficiencies, Agile Leaders can identify areas for improvement and implement changes accordingly. The emphasis on iterative feedback loops enables teams to learn from their experiences and make incremental adjustments for better outcomes over time.

However, like any other framework, there are potential drawbacks associated with implementing Enterprise Kanban as well. One challenge lies in striking the right balance between flexibility and structure. While adaptability is crucial in an ever-changing environment, too much flexibility can lead to chaos and an inability to meet deadlines. Agile Leaders must find the sweet spot where teams have enough freedom to respond to changes while maintaining a level of structure that ensures progress.

Another consideration is the need for proper training and understanding of Enterprise Kanban principles. Without adequate knowledge and buy-in from all team members, there is a risk of misinterpretation or partial adoption, resulting in suboptimal outcomes. Agile Leaders should invest time in educating their teams about the framework's core concepts, ensuring everyone understands its purpose and benefits.

To effectively implement Enterprise Kanban, Agile Leaders should follow a few key steps. Firstly, they should assess their organization's readiness for adopting this framework. This includes evaluating current workflows, identifying pain points, and determining the level of commitment from stakeholders. A thorough assessment will provide valuable insights into potential challenges and enable leaders to address them proactively.

Next, Agile Leaders should design an Enterprise Kanban system tailored specifically to their organization's needs. This involves mapping out workflows, defining work item types, establishing policies for task prioritization, and creating visual boards that reflect the unique characteristics of the organization's work processes. Customizing the system ensures it aligns with existing structures and encourages widespread adoption across teams.

Once implemented, Agile Leaders must actively monitor the Enterprise Kanban system to ensure its effectiveness. Regular reviews help identify areas for improvement or adjustments needed in response to changing circumstances. By collecting data on cycle times, lead times, and throughput rates across different stages of work completion, leaders can make data-driven decisions that optimize workflow efficiency.

Enterprise Kanban offers numerous benefits for Agile Leaders seeking a flexible yet structured approach to managing work at an organizational level. By embracing this framework's power and leveraging its principles effectively, leaders can enhance transparency within their organizations while promoting collaboration and continuous improvement. While challenges may arise along the way, with proper training and a thoughtful implementation strategy, Agile Leaders can harness the full potential of Enterprise Kanban to achieve their goals and drive organizational success.

thirty-seven

The Value Stream

As an agile leader, understanding the concept of value streams is crucial to your success. In this chapter, we will explore what value streams are, how they differ from traditional project management, and the immense benefits they can bring to your organization.

Value streams can be defined as the end-to-end flow of activities required to deliver a product or service to a customer. They provide a holistic view of the entire process, from idea generation to product delivery. By mapping out these value streams, leaders gain valuable insights into areas that need improvement, bottlenecks that hinder progress, and opportunities for optimization.

Value stream mapping is a technique used to visualize and analyze these value streams. It involves creating a detailed map that captures each step in the process, including inputs, outputs, and handoffs between different teams or departments. This mapping exercise helps identify waste, redundancies, and inefficiencies within the system.

One of the key differences between value streams and traditional project management lies in their focus. While project management tends to be task-oriented and focuses on individual projects or initiatives, value streams take a broader perspective by considering all interconnected activities within an organization. This shift in mindset allows leaders to see beyond isolated projects and optimize their entire workflow.

By adopting value streams in their organization's leadership practices, agile leaders unlock several benefits. Firstly, it enables them to prioritize work based on customer needs rather than individual projects' requirements. This customer-centric approach ensures that efforts are aligned with delivering maximum value while minimizing waste.

Moreover, by visualizing end-to-end processes through value stream mapping exercises regularly conducted by leaders in collaboration with teams across departments - organizations gain transparency into their operations like never before! This increased visibility helps identify areas for improvement promptly and facilitates data-driven decision-making.

Another advantage of embracing value streams is improved collaboration among teams across different functional areas. Since everyone understands how their work contributes to achieving overall goals, silos are broken down, and cross-functional collaboration becomes the norm. This collaborative environment fosters innovation and encourages teams to share best practices, leading to increased efficiency and higher-quality outcomes.

Additionally, value streams promote a culture of continuous improvement within organizations. By regularly reviewing and analyzing value stream maps, leaders can identify bottlenecks or inefficiencies that hinder productivity. This insight enables them to implement targeted improvements, optimize processes, and reduce waste systematically.

One such improvement technique often used in conjunction with value streams is known as Kaizen. Kaizen involves making small incremental changes consistently over time to drive continuous improvement. By incorporating Kaizen into their leadership practices, agile leaders create an environment where everyone is encouraged to contribute ideas for improvement regularly.

Value streams offer agile leaders a powerful toolset for driving organizational success. By understanding the concept of value streams and leveraging techniques like value stream mapping, leaders gain valuable insights into their organization's end-to-end processes. Through this holistic perspective, they can prioritize work based on customer needs and optimize workflow efficiency—all while fostering collaboration among teams across different functional areas.

Moreover, by embracing a culture of continuous improvement through regular reviews of value stream maps and implementing incremental changes using techniques like Kaizen—agile leaders create an environment that drives sustainable growth and success.

thirty-eight

Business Agility

The ability to adapt and respond quickly is crucial for survival. This is where Business Agility comes into play - a concept that parallels the agility of a medical doctor in diagnosing and treating patients. Just as doctors need to be agile in their decision-making process to provide the best care, leaders too must embrace Business Agility to ensure their organizations thrive.

Business Agility can be defined as the ability of an organization to rapidly respond and adapt to market changes, customer needs, and emerging trends. It goes beyond mere flexibility; it requires a proactive mindset that seeks continuous improvement and innovation. By embracing Business Agility, companies can stay one step ahead of their competitors while delivering exceptional value to their customers.

One of the key goals of Business Agility is Customer Centricity. In today's highly competitive marketplace, organizations must prioritize understanding their customers' needs and expectations. By doing so, they can tailor their products or services accordingly, ensuring customer satisfaction and loyalty.

Leadership plays a critical role in fostering Business Agility within organizations. They are responsible for setting the tone at the top and creating an environment that encourages agility throughout all levels of the company. Effective leaders understand that agility starts with them - they must embrace change themselves before expecting others to do so.

To foster Business Agility within an organization, leaders should focus on three key components: culture, processes, and people.

Culture:

Creating a culture that values innovation, collaboration, and continuous learning is essential for building agility. Leaders should encourage open communication channels where ideas are freely shared without fear of judgment or reprisal. By nurturing a culture that rewards experimentation rather than punishing failure, leaders can unleash the creative potential within their teams.

Processes:

Traditional hierarchical structures often hinder agility by slowing down decision-making processes. Leaders should adopt agile frameworks such as Scrum or Kanban to streamline workflows and promote cross-functional collaboration. These frameworks emphasize iterative and incremental progress, allowing teams to adapt quickly to changing circumstances. By implementing lean processes, leaders can eliminate waste and optimize efficiency.

People:

People are the heart of any organization, and their skills and mindset can make or break agility. Leaders should invest in their employees' development through training programs, coaching, and mentorship. They should empower their teams to make decisions independently while providing guidance and support when needed. By nurturing a growth mindset within the workforce, leaders can cultivate a culture of continuous improvement that fuels Business Agility.

Business Agility is vital for organizations striving to thrive in today's dynamic business environment. Just as medical doctors must be agile in diagnosing and treating patients, business leaders must embrace agility to stay competitive. By focusing on Customer Centricity, fostering an agile culture, implementing streamlined processes, and investing in people's growth, leaders can pave the way for Business Agility within their organizations.

thirty-nine

Design Thinking

Design Thinking is a powerful tool that can greatly benefit agile organizations. In this chapter, we will explore what Design Thinking is and how it can be utilized to support and enhance agility. We will also delve into the crucial role of leadership in fostering and nurturing Design Thinking within an organization.

At its core, Design Thinking is a human-centered approach to problem-solving. It focuses on understanding the needs, desires, and challenges of the people who will be impacted by a particular product or service. By empathizing with users and stakeholders, Design Thinking allows for innovative solutions that truly meet their needs.

In an agile context, Design Thinking plays a pivotal role in ensuring that products or services are developed with a deep understanding of the end-users' requirements. Agile organizations embrace iterative development cycles, where feedback from users is continuously incorporated into the product design process. Design Thinking acts as the guiding principle for this iterative feedback loop.

The first step in applying Design Thinking within an agile organization is to define the problem at hand. This involves engaging with stakeholders and gaining a comprehensive understanding of their pain points, desires, and aspirations. By actively listening to stakeholders' perspectives, leaders can gain valuable insights that inform problem definition.

Once the problem has been defined, leaders need to encourage cross-functional collaboration among teams responsible for product development. In an agile environment, multidisciplinary teams work together to brainstorm ideas and potential solutions. This collaborative approach fosters creativity and brings diverse perspectives into play.

The next step involves ideation – generating as many ideas as possible without judgment or criticism. Leaders must create an environment where team members feel comfortable contributing their thoughts freely. It is through this open exchange of ideas that breakthrough innovations often emerge.

After ideation comes prototyping – transforming ideas into tangible representations that can be tested by end-users. Prototypes serve as low-fidelity models that allow teams to gather valuable feedback early in the development process without investing significant time and resources. By involving end-users in the prototyping stage, leaders ensure that their needs and preferences are considered from the outset.

Testing and iteration form the next phase of Design Thinking. Leaders need to instill a culture of experimentation within their agile organizations, where failure is seen as a stepping stone to improvement. By embracing a fail-fast mentality, teams can quickly identify flaws or areas for enhancement and make necessary adjustments.

Throughout this process, leaders play a crucial role in supporting Design Thinking within their organizations. They must foster an environment where creativity and innovation thrive by empowering their teams to take risks and explore new ideas. Moreover, leaders need to lead by example, demonstrating a willingness to learn from failures and adapt accordingly.

Leaders should also champion user-centricity by emphasizing the importance of understanding end-users' perspectives. By encouraging empathy among team members, leaders pave the way for solutions that truly resonate with users' needs.

In addition to nurturing Design Thinking within their teams, leaders must also ensure alignment with organizational goals. They need to communicate the strategic vision behind adopting Design Thinking principles and highlight how it aligns with agile methodologies. This clarity of purpose helps create buy-in from all levels of the organization.

By integrating Design Thinking into agile practices, organizations can reap numerous benefits. It allows them to develop products that genuinely meet users' needs while fostering innovation through continuous feedback loops. Furthermore, it empowers teams by providing them with a structured approach to problem-solving that inspires creativity.

Design Thinking is an invaluable tool for agile organizations seeking to enhance their problem-solving capabilities while staying aligned with end-users' needs. Leadership plays a vital role in supporting Design Thinking by fostering collaboration, encouraging experimentation, and championing user-centricity. By embracing this human-centered approach, agile leaders can propel their organizations toward greater success in an ever-evolving world of complexity.

forty

Lean Portfolio Management

In this chapter, we will delve into the concept of Lean Portfolio Management (LPM) and explore its significance in an organization. We will discuss the composition of the LPM team, their interactions with various stakeholders, the role they play within the organization, and how to successfully implement a Lean Portfolio Management team.

Lean Portfolio Management is a strategic approach that enables organizations to align their portfolios with business objectives and optimize value delivery. It encompasses a set of principles and practices that help organizations make informed investment decisions, prioritize work, and ensure effective execution.

The LPM team consists of individuals who possess a deep understanding of agile methodologies and are responsible for managing the portfolio in an agile manner. This team typically includes representatives from different departments such as product management, finance, marketing, IT operations, and project management. The diversity within the team ensures that all perspectives are considered when making decisions related to portfolio investments.

Interaction with stakeholders is vital for the success of LPM. The LPM team collaborates closely with executives, business owners, product managers, scrum masters, agile coaches, architects, and other key stakeholders to gather insights into market trends, customer needs, and organizational goals. By involving these stakeholders in decision-making processes early on, LPM fosters transparency and facilitates buy-in from all parties involved.

The role of Lean Portfolio Management within an organization is multifaceted. Firstly, it serves as a bridge between strategy formulation at an executive level and execution at an operational level. The LPM team ensures that strategic objectives are broken down into actionable initiatives that can be implemented by Agile Release Trains (ARTs) or teams working on specific projects or products.

Secondly, LPM provides visibility into portfolio performance by utilizing key performance indicators (KPIs) that measure progress toward strategic goals. By regularly monitoring these KPIs, the LPM team can identify areas where adjustments or reallocation of resources may be necessary to maximize value delivery.

Moreover, LPM plays a crucial role in fostering a culture of continuous improvement within an organization. By regularly reviewing and evaluating the performance of initiatives, the LPM team can identify bottlenecks, dependencies, and areas for improvement. This enables them to make data-driven decisions that optimize the portfolio's overall performance.

Implementing a Lean Portfolio Management team requires careful planning and execution. Here are some steps to consider when establishing LPM within your organization:

1. **Define Goals:**

Clearly articulate your organization's strategic goals and align them with your portfolio objectives. This will provide a clear direction for the LPM team to follow.

1. **Form the Team:**

Assemble a diverse group of individuals with expertise in agile methodologies and various business functions. Ensure that each member understands their role within the team and how they contribute to achieving organizational goals.

1. **Establish Governance:**

Develop governance mechanisms that define decision-making processes, roles, responsibilities, and escalation paths within the LPM team. This will ensure accountability and transparency throughout portfolio management activities.

1. **Create Portfolio Kanban:**

Implement a visual representation of your portfolio using Kanban boards or similar tools. This will help track initiatives from ideation to implementation and provide visibility into their progress.

1. **Prioritize Work:**

Use techniques such as Weighted Shortest Job First (WSJF) or Cost of Delay (CoD) to prioritize work based on business value, risk factors, dependencies, and time sensitivity.

1. **Monitor Performance:**

Define KPIs that align with strategic objectives and regularly review them to measure progress towards goals. Adjust priorities or reallocate resources as necessary based on these performance indicators.

1. **Continuous Improvement:**

Foster a culture of continuous improvement by conducting regular retrospectives at both individual initiative level as well as overall portfolio level. Encourage feedback from all stakeholders involved in the process.

By implementing Lean Portfolio Management practices effectively, organizations can streamline their portfolio management processes, ensure alignment with business objectives, and deliver maximum value to their customers. The LPM team acts as the catalyst for this transformation, bringing together diverse perspectives and facilitating collaboration across the organization.

forty-one

Lean Agile Center of Excellence

As organizations strive to embrace agility and adaptability, the concept of a Lean Agile Center of Excellence has emerged as a pivotal element in their transformation journey. This chapter delves into the intricacies of this center, shedding light on its purpose, structure, and the crucial role it plays within an organization.

The Lean Agile Center of Excellence serves as a guiding force, ensuring that agile principles are effectively implemented throughout the organization. It acts as a nucleus for driving change and fostering continuous improvement. But what exactly is this center, and who should be part of it?

At its core, a Lean Agile Center of Excellence is comprised of seasoned individuals who possess deep expertise in agile methodologies and practices. These individuals are not only well-versed in the technical aspects but also have a profound understanding of the cultural transformation required to fully embrace agility.

Forming such a center requires careful consideration. Organizations typically select cross-functional team members from various departments - individuals who exhibit strong leadership skills and have previously demonstrated their dedication to driving change. By bringing together professionals from diverse backgrounds, an environment conducive to innovation and collaboration is fostered.

The establishment of a Lean Agile Center of Excellence follows various approaches depending on the organizational context. Some organizations opt for an evolutionary approach where existing agile teams gradually form the nucleus of this center. Others prefer a more deliberate approach where individuals are specifically chosen based on their expertise and track record.

Regardless of how it is formed, the responsibilities bestowed upon this center are critical to ensuring success in organizational agility. One primary responsibility lies in providing guidance and support to teams across different departments throughout their agile journey. This involves coaching teams on agile practices, facilitating training sessions, and nurturing an environment that encourages knowledge sharing.

Moreover, the Lean Agile Center of Excellence serves as a custodian for maintaining consistency in adopting agile frameworks across projects within the organization. They establish standardized processes that align with agile principles while allowing for flexibility and adaptation to specific project needs. By providing these guidelines, the center promotes a harmonized approach and avoids fragmented implementations.

The center's role extends beyond coaching and standardization; it also acts as a catalyst for continuous improvement. By regularly assessing the organization's agile maturity, identifying areas of improvement, and suggesting relevant strategies, this center ensures that agility becomes deeply ingrained in the organizational DNA.

To effectively fulfill their responsibilities, members of the Lean Agile Center of Excellence must possess strong leadership qualities. They need to inspire change, influence stakeholders across all levels of the organization, and advocate for agile principles. Their ability to navigate through resistance and skepticism plays a pivotal role in driving successful transformation initiatives.

A Lean Agile Center of Excellence is an indispensable element in an organization's journey toward agility. Its formation involves carefully selecting individuals with deep expertise in agile practices while ensuring cross-functional representation. This center serves as a guiding force that provides support, guidance, standardization, and continuous improvement opportunities throughout the organization.

Much like skilled medical doctors who diagnose ailments accurately and prescribe appropriate treatments with precision, the members of this center diagnose organizational inefficiencies accurately and prescribe agile methodologies tailored to each department's needs. They are adept at understanding not only the technical aspects but also the cultural shifts required to bring about lasting change.

As we embark on our journey towards becoming agile leaders within our organizations, let us recognize the significance of establishing a Lean Agile Center of Excellence. By doing so, we lay a solid foundation upon which sustainable agility can flourish - one that will elevate not just our organizations but also ourselves as leaders who can adapt swiftly to meet any challenge that comes our way.

forty-two

SecDevOps Leadership

Implementing and Supporting SecDevOps Leadership

The need for secure and efficient software development has become paramount. As an Agile leader, it is crucial to understand the importance of SecDevOps (Security Development Operations) and how it can be implemented and supported within your organization. This chapter will delve into current trends, pitfalls, and solutions associated with SecDevOps leadership.

SecDevOps is the integration of security practices into the DevOps process, ensuring that security measures are implemented throughout the entire software development lifecycle. It aims to bridge the gap between development teams and security teams by fostering collaboration, communication, and automation. By embedding security early on in the development process, organizations can proactively address vulnerabilities and prevent potential threats.

One of the key trends in SecDevOps leadership is shifting from a reactive to a proactive approach. Traditionally, security measures were often an afterthought in software development projects. However, this approach leaves organizations vulnerable to cyberattacks or breaches. Agile leaders must recognize that security needs to be a primary concern from day one of any project.

To effectively implement SecDevOps within your organization, it is essential to establish a culture of collaboration between developers and security professionals. Breaking down silos between these two teams enables them to work together seamlessly towards common goals. Regular meetings where both parties can exchange ideas and insights are vital for fostering this collaborative environment.

Automation plays a pivotal role in supporting SecDevOps initiatives. By automating security testing processes such as code scanning or vulnerability assessments, organizations can ensure consistent application of best practices across all projects. Automated tools provide real-time feedback on potential vulnerabilities or weaknesses in codebases while enabling developers to fix issues promptly.

While implementing SecDevOps may seem like a straightforward process on paper, there are several pitfalls that Agile leaders must navigate carefully. One common challenge is resistance from developers who perceive additional security measures as roadblocks to their productivity. To overcome this, leaders should emphasize the importance of security in delivering reliable and trusted products. Education and training on secure coding practices can also help developers understand the long-term benefits of incorporating security into their workflows.

Another pitfall is overlooking the human element in SecDevOps. While automation plays a significant role, it cannot replace human intuition and expertise. Agile leaders must ensure that security professionals are involved throughout the development process, providing guidance and oversight where necessary. By fostering a strong relationship between developers and security experts, organizations can strike the right balance between agility and robustness.

To address these challenges, several solutions have emerged in the realm of SecDevOps leadership. One such solution is implementing a secure coding framework that provides developers with guidelines and best practices for writing secure code. This empowers developers to proactively address security concerns while maintaining their productivity.

Continuous monitoring is another crucial aspect of successful SecDevOps implementation. By continuously monitoring applications for potential vulnerabilities or breaches, organizations can respond rapidly to any threats or incidents that arise. This real-time visibility allows Agile leaders to make informed decisions based on current data.

SecDevOps has become an indispensable component of software development in today's digital landscape. Agile leaders must embrace this paradigm shift by implementing and supporting SecDevOps within their organizations effectively. By fostering collaboration, embracing automation, addressing common pitfalls, and leveraging emerging solutions, organizations can build robust software systems that not only meet business requirements but also prioritize security from inception to deployment

forty-three

Agile Career Paths

Navigating Agile Career Paths

There are numerous paths one can embark upon to build a successful career. Whether you are new to the field or looking to advance your current position, this chapter will serve as your compass, guiding you through the various options and opportunities that lie before you.

Starting your journey in the agile field can be an exciting yet overwhelming experience. The first step is often determining where to begin. For those just stepping into this world, a good starting point is often as a Scrum Master or an Agile Coach.

As a Scrum Master, you will play a crucial role in facilitating communication and collaboration within an Agile team. You will guide team members in adhering to Scrum principles and practices, ensuring that projects stay on track and obstacles are swiftly addressed. To succeed in this role, it takes strong facilitation skills, empathy towards team members' needs, and a deep understanding of Agile frameworks.

On the other hand, becoming an Agile Coach allows you to take on a broader perspective. As an advocate for Agile principles at both the team and organizational levels, your primary focus will be on fostering continuous improvement and driving cultural change within the company. This role demands excellent coaching skills, strong leadership abilities, and a knack for navigating complex organizational dynamics.

Once you have gained experience as either a Scrum Master or an Agile Coach, doors will open up to other exciting career paths within the Agile realm. One such path is that of an Agile Project Manager.

As an Agile Project Manager, you will oversee project planning and execution using Agile methodologies. You will ensure that project objectives are met while maintaining flexibility in responding to changing requirements. This role requires exceptional organizational skills along with the ability to adapt quickly in dynamic environments.

For those with technical expertise who wish to remain hands-on while leading teams toward agility, becoming an Engineering Lead or DevOps Engineer could be the path to follow. In these roles, you will combine your technical prowess with Agile practices to drive the development and delivery of high-quality software products. Success in these positions relies on strong technical skills, a passion for innovation, and the ability to inspire and guide others.

As you progress in your career, leadership opportunities will arise that allow you to influence not only projects but also entire organizations. The role of an Agile Transformation Lead or an Agile Coach at the enterprise level is one such opportunity.

In these positions, you will be responsible for driving the adoption of Agile principles across multiple teams and departments. You will serve as a change agent, guiding organizations through their agile transformation journey. To excel in these roles, you must possess exceptional communication skills, strategic thinking abilities, and a deep understanding of organizational dynamics.

It is essential to note that while each path has its own unique set of responsibilities and demands, they all share common attributes required for success. These include excellent communication skills, adaptability to change, a continuous learning mindset, collaboration abilities, and a passion for empowering teams.

As you navigate your agile career path journey, it is crucial to identify areas where you can continue growing both professionally and personally. Seek out opportunities for further education and certifications in Agile methodologies such as Certified ScrumMaster (CSM), Certified Scrum Product Owner (CSPO), or Scaled Agile Framework (SAFe) certifications.

Remember that agility is not limited solely to one's job title or position within an organization; it is a mindset that can be applied across various industries and roles. Embrace opportunities for growth outside your comfort zone and seek mentorship from experienced agile practitioners who can guide you along your path.

The world of agile offers diverse career paths filled with exciting challenges and opportunities for growth. Whether starting as a Scrum Master or aiming for leadership positions at an enterprise level - there is no shortage of possibilities awaiting those who embrace agility wholeheartedly. So, take the plunge, be open to new experiences, and let your agile journey unfold before you.

forty-four

How Many Coaches, Scrum Masters and Product Owners?

Determining the Right Number of Agile Coaches, Scrum Masters, and Product Owners

In the previous chapters, we have explored the many roles we might take on in our Agile Career path. Now, it is time to delve into a crucial aspect of leading an organization toward agility - determining how many of these roles are needed within your specific context.

The number of agile coaches, scrum masters, and product owners required can vary significantly depending on the maturity level of your organization and its teams. In less mature organizations that are just starting their agile journey, having more people in these roles might be necessary to provide guidance and support. As organizations become more experienced with agile practices and principles, they tend to require fewer individuals in these roles as teams become self-sufficient.

However, leaders need to understand that everyone within the organization should consider themselves as agile coaches. Agile leadership is not limited to a select few; it should be embraced by all individuals at every level. While dedicated coaches can offer specialized expertise and guidance, fostering a culture where everyone takes ownership of their role as an agile leader is crucial for long-term success.

One question that often arises when considering hiring agile coaches is whether they should be internal employees or temporary consultants. Both options have their pros and cons. Internal employees have a deeper understanding of the organization's culture and processes but can sometimes struggle with objectivity due to their vested interests. On the other hand, temporary consultants bring fresh perspectives from outside the organization but may take longer to integrate into the team dynamics.

To make an informed decision about hiring internal employees or consultants as agile coaches, leaders should carefully assess their organization's specific needs. Consider factors such as existing team dynamics, available resources for training and development if internal employees are chosen, or budget constraints if consultants are preferred.

It is important to note that in recent years the market for agile coaching has become saturated with individuals claiming to be experts with little experience. This influx of inexperienced coaches can hinder an organization's agile transformation efforts. When hiring agile coaches, it is crucial to be mindful that quality often comes at a higher price. Investing in experienced and knowledgeable coaches can significantly impact the success of your organization's agile journey.

To ensure accountability and measure progress towards agility, it is essential to have a robust assessment mechanism in place. Assessments such as Comparative Agility offer valuable insights into an organization's progress and provide a benchmark against which improvements can be tracked. By regularly measuring and reporting on progress, leaders can hold agile coaches, scrum masters, and product owners accountable for their contributions to the organization's agility.

Determining the right number of agile coaches, scrum masters, and product owners requires careful consideration of your organization's maturity level and specific needs. While having dedicated individuals in these roles can provide valuable support and expertise, fostering a culture where everyone embraces their role as an agile leader is equally important. Whether you choose internal employees or consultants as agile coaches, prioritize experience over cost to ensure the best possible outcomes for your organization's agile transformation journey. Finally, measuring progress through assessments like Comparative Agility will enable you to track your organization's growth toward agility effectively.

By taking these factors into account when determining the number of agile coaches, scrum masters, and product owners needed within your organization, you are laying a solid foundation for success on your path toward becoming an Agile Leader.

forty-five

How Do I Know if Agile is For Me?

Finding Your Fit in Agile

When embarking on a career path, it is essential to assess whether the chosen field aligns with your skills, interests, and values. The realm of Agile methodology is no exception. In this chapter, we will explore how you can self-reflect on whether a career in Agile is the right fit for you. We will also discuss alternative roles that leverage your experience as a Scrum Master or Agile Coach if you wish to explore new horizons.

Assessing Your Compatibility:

Before diving into an Agile career, it is crucial to understand the reasons behind your dissatisfaction with your current role. Is it because of the inherent characteristics of an agile role or due to struggles within your organization's implementation of agile practices?

Take some time for introspection and consider the following questions:

1. Do you thrive in dynamic environments?

Agile methodologies are built upon adaptability and constant change. If you enjoy being proactive in embracing uncertainty and are energized by fast-paced work environments, then pursuing an Agile career might be a natural fit for you.

2. Are you comfortable with collaboration?

Agile emphasizes teamwork and cross-functional collaboration. If you find joy in working closely with diverse individuals, facilitating effective communication, and fostering camaraderie among team members, then an Agile role could be highly rewarding for you.

3. How do you handle ambiguity?

In Agile projects, requirements evolve continuously, leaving room for interpretation and adaptation. If ambiguity excites rather than frustrates you and if problem-solving under uncertain circumstances invigorates your passion for work, then Agile may provide the ideal playground for your talents.

4. Are continuous learning and improvement part of your DNA?

Agile thrives on a growth mindset that encourages ongoing learning from both successes and failures. If you possess an insatiable thirst for knowledge and constantly seek opportunities to enhance yourself personally and professionally, then pursuing a career in Agile will provide you with a fertile ground for development.

Exploring Alternative Roles:

If, upon reflection, you discover that Agile may not be the best fit for you, fear not! Your experience as a Scrum Master or Agile Coach equips you with valuable skills that can be leveraged in various other roles.

Consider the following options:

1. Project Manager:

Your expertise in facilitating communication, managing teams, and ensuring project success makes transitioning into a project management role a logical step. With your understanding of Agile methodologies, you can bridge the gap between traditional project management practices and more adaptive approaches.

2. Product Owner:

As an Agile Coach or Scrum Master, you have gained firsthand insights into product development processes. Leveraging this knowledge can make transitioning into a Product Owner role seamless. Your ability to understand customer needs and steer product direction aligns perfectly with this vital role within an Agile team.

3. Change Management Consultant:

Agile transformations often require change management expertise to navigate organizational shifts successfully. Your experience as an Agile Coach gives you a solid foundation in guiding teams through change and transforming mindsets. Transitioning to a change management consultant role allows you to apply these skills across different industries and organizations.

4. Training and Development Specialist:

Your proficiency in coaching and mentoring individuals can be applied beyond the realm of software development projects. Transitioning into a training and development specialist role enables you to share your knowledge and empower others within various domains, helping them embrace agility beyond software development.

In Summary:

Determining whether an Agile career is right for you requires introspection and honest self-assessment of your preferences, strengths, and goals. By reflecting on your compatibility with agile principles such as collaboration, adaptability, embracing ambiguity, and continuous improvement, you can make an informed decision about pursuing an Agile career or exploring alternative roles that best leverage your skills acquired as a Scrum Master or Agile Coach.

Remember that finding the perfect fit may involve trial and error, and it's okay to explore different paths. Embrace the journey of self-discovery, and may it lead you to a career that brings you fulfillment, growth, and the opportunity to make a positive impact in your chosen field.

forty-six

The Agile Coach

Agile Coaching Reflection and Transitioning

As an Agile Coach, it is essential to periodically reflect on your impact and effectiveness within the Agile community. Are you truly contributing to the overall good, or are there aspects of your coaching style that may be inadvertently harming teams and organizations? This chapter delves into the importance of self-awareness and explores alternative roles that may be a better fit for individuals who find themselves questioning their suitability as an Agile Coach.

The Role of an Agile Coach

Being an Agile Coach demands a unique set of skills and qualities. It requires the ability to guide teams through the complexities of agile methodologies, foster collaboration, and facilitate continuous improvement. However, not everyone is cut out for this role, despite their best intentions. It is crucial to recognize when being an Agile Coach may not be a good fit.

Signs that Agile Coaching May Not Be Right for You

1. Lack of Passion:

If you find yourself lacking enthusiasm or passion for guiding teams toward agility, it might be time to reevaluate your career choice. Passion is contagious, and without it, your coaching effectiveness may diminish.

2. Resistance to Change:

As an Agile Coach, you must embrace change as a foundational principle. If you find yourself resisting change or struggling with adapting to new approaches, it could hinder your ability to effectively coach teams in their agile journey.

3. Inflexibility:

Agility demands flexibility from both teams and coaches alike. If you possess a rigid mindset or struggle with adapting your coaching style based on team dynamics or organizational needs, it may limit your effectiveness in driving positive change.

4. Lack of Empathy:

Successful coaching requires empathy—an ability to understand others' perspectives and tailor guidance accordingly. Without empathy, it becomes challenging to connect with team members on a deeper level and address their unique challenges effectively.5. Burnout: The demanding nature of being an Agile Coach can lead to burnout if proper self-care and boundaries are not established. If you consistently feel overwhelmed, exhausted, or disillusioned with the role, it may be an indication that a change is necessary.

Exploring Alternative Roles

Recognizing that Agile Coaching may not align with your strengths or interests does not mean the end of your agile journey. Numerous alternative roles within the agile community offer new avenues for growth and contribution.

Consider these alternatives:

1. Scrum Master:

As a Scrum Master, you can focus on guiding one specific team in their adoption of agile practices. This role allows for a more concentrated effort in facilitating team dynamics and ensuring adherence to scrum principles.

2. Product Owner:

If you possess strong business acumen and enjoy strategic decision-making, becoming a Product Owner might be an ideal transition. As a Product Owner, you would focus on maximizing product value and working closely with stakeholders to define product vision and priorities.

3. Agile Project Manager:

For those who thrive in managing projects while embracing agile principles, transitioning into an Agile Project Manager role could be the perfect fit. This position requires overseeing project execution while promoting collaboration and adaptive planning.

4. Agile Trainer:

If your passion lies in sharing knowledge and helping others embrace agility, becoming an Agile Trainer could be an excellent choice. This role involves conducting training sessions, workshops, and coaching sessions to empower individuals and organizations on their agile journey.

Final Thoughts

Agile Coaching is a challenging but rewarding career path for those who possess the necessary skills and mindset. However, it's essential to periodically assess if this role aligns with your aspirations and abilities as circumstances evolve.

If you find yourself questioning your effectiveness as an Agile Coach or notice signs indicating it may not be the right fit for you anymore, don't despair—there are alternative roles within the Agile community that can leverage your strengths while providing new growth opportunities.

Remember that self-awareness is key; being honest with yourself about your passions, strengths, and limitations will ultimately lead you to a fulfilling and impactful role within the agile community. Embrace the journey of self-discovery and transition, for it is through these moments that we continue to grow as individuals and professionals.

forty-seven

Continuous Learning of Ways of Working

As an agile leader, it is essential to continuously expand and enhance your knowledge and skills in agile and modern ways of working. In this chapter, we will explore various avenues through which you can achieve this goal. By engaging in continuous learning, you will stay at the forefront of industry trends and ensure that you are equipped with the necessary tools to lead effectively.

Books are an excellent resource for learning about agile methodologies and their practical implementation. There are several noteworthy books, in addition to the one you are currently reading, available that delve into different aspects of agile leadership. Some highly recommended titles include "Scrum: The Art of Doing Twice the Work in Half the Time" by Jeff Sutherland, "The Lean Startup" by Eric Ries, and "The Agile Leader: How to Create an Agile Business in the Digital Age" by Simon Hartley. These books provide valuable insights into Agile practices, enabling you to deepen your understanding and apply them in your work environment.

In addition to books, local networking communities offer a wealth of knowledge-sharing opportunities. These communities consist of like-minded individuals who gather regularly to discuss agile methodologies, share experiences, and learn from one another. By participating actively in these communities, you can gain insights from fellow practitioners who have faced similar challenges or discovered innovative solutions. Look for local meetups or online forums dedicated to agile leadership within your area; these platforms serve as valuable resources for fostering connections with other professionals passionate about Agile practices.

Agile conferences present another invaluable opportunity for continuous learning. Attending global conferences such as the Global SAFe Summit allows you to immerse yourself in a rich environment filled with thought leaders, industry experts, and practitioners from around the world. These events often feature keynote speeches by renowned speakers who share their experiences and insights on leading Agile transformations successfully.

On a domestic level, conferences like Agile Midwest offer a platform for intensive learning within regional settings. Such conferences bring together professionals from nearby areas, allowing for targeted discussions on specific challenges faced in a particular context. By attending these conferences, you can gain a deeper understanding of the nuances and intricacies involved in implementing Agile methodologies within your region.

Agile open spaces are another excellent avenue for continuous learning. These self-organizing events provide an open forum for participants to discuss topics of interest, share experiences, and collaborate on finding solutions to common problems. The agenda is determined by the attendees themselves, ensuring that the discussions revolve around relevant and pressing issues. Engaging in agile open spaces enables you to tap into the collective wisdom of diverse individuals who bring various perspectives and experiences to the table.

In addition to these specific avenues, it is crucial to cultivate a mindset of continuous learning in your day-to-day activities as an agile leader. Actively seek out opportunities to expand your knowledge by reading articles, following industry blogs, or engaging in online courses that focus on Agile practices or related disciplines such as Lean or DevOps. Embrace feedback from your team members and encourage a culture of learning within your organization.

By continuously expanding and enhancing your knowledge and skills in agile ways of working, you not only benefit yourself but also create an environment conducive to growth within your team. This commitment to continuous learning sets you apart as an agile leader who remains adaptable and responsive to changing market dynamics.

AGILE RX: A PRESCRIPTION TO GUIDE AGILE LEADERS

In this chapter, we explored various avenues for continuous learning in agile leadership. From books and local networking communities to global conferences and agile open spaces, each avenue offers unique opportunities for growth and development. As an agile leader committed to excellence, embrace these opportunities with enthusiasm and curiosity—always seeking new ways to enhance your understanding of modern ways of working. Through continuous learning, you will become a masterful leader capable of guiding your team toward success in today's rapidly evolving business landscape.

forty-eight

Modern Ways of Working

Embrace.

In today's rapidly evolving world, staying ahead of the curve is crucial for success. The traditional ways of working are no longer sufficient to meet the demands of a fast-paced and ever-changing landscape. In this chapter, we will explore the emerging modern ways of working and how individuals can acquire the necessary skills and experience to thrive in this new era.

1. Agile Methodology:

While it has been around for decades, Agile is still a modern way of work due to its ever-changing ways that we learn to utilize it. Originally developed for software development, Agile principles have now expanded into various industries and sectors. The key idea behind Agile is to break down complex projects into smaller, manageable tasks called sprints. By embracing iterative processes, continuous collaboration, and frequent feedback loops, teams can adapt quickly to changing requirements and deliver high-quality results.

2. Remote Work:

Another modern way of working that has become increasingly prevalent is remote work or telecommuting. Technological advancements have made it possible for individuals to work from anywhere in the world as long as they have an internet connection. Remote work offers numerous benefits such as increased flexibility, improved work-life balance, reduced commuting time, and access to a global talent pool.

3. Cross-functional Teams:

Traditional hierarchical structures are being replaced by cross-functional teams in many organizations today. These teams consist of members with diverse skill sets who collaborate across departments to achieve common goals. By bringing together individuals with different perspectives and expertise, cross-functional teams foster innovation, creativity, and higher levels of productivity.

4. Continuous Learning:

With rapid advancements in technology and industry practices, continuous learning has become essential for professionals looking to stay relevant in their fields. Modern ways of working require individuals to embrace a growth mindset and actively seek opportunities for acquiring new knowledge and skills through online courses, workshops, conferences, or professional networks.

5. Design Thinking:

Design thinking is an approach that emphasizes empathy towards end-users while solving complex problems. It involves understanding the needs and desires of users, brainstorming creative solutions, prototyping, and testing. By adopting a design thinking mindset, individuals can tackle challenges from a human-centered perspective, leading to innovative and user-friendly outcomes.

To acquire the skills and experience needed to embrace these modern ways of working, individuals can explore various avenues:

1. Professional Development Programs:

Many organizations offer professional development programs designed to equip employees with the necessary skills for modern ways of working. These programs may include training sessions, mentorship opportunities, or access to online learning platforms.

2. Online Learning Platforms:

The internet provides an abundance of resources for individuals seeking to upskill themselves. Online learning platforms like Udemy, Coursera, or LinkedIn Learning offer a wide range of courses on topics such as Agile methodology, remote work best practices, cross-functional collaboration techniques or design thinking principles.

3. Networking and Collaboration:

Building strong professional networks is crucial for staying informed about emerging trends in modern ways of working. Engaging with like-minded professionals through industry conferences or online communities allows individuals to learn from others' experiences and exchange ideas that can enhance their practices.

4. Experimentation and Reflection:

To truly embrace modern ways of working, individuals should be open to experimentation and willing to reflect on their experiences regularly. Trying new approaches in small increments allows for iterative improvement while reflecting on successes and failures helps identify areas for growth.

Embracing modern ways of working is essential in today's dynamic world. Agile methodology encourages flexibility and adaptability; remote work offers increased freedom; cross-functional teams foster collaboration; continuous learning ensures relevance; design thinking promotes innovation - all are valuable tools that enable professionals to thrive amidst constant change.

By actively seeking opportunities for growth through professional development programs, online learning platforms networking events, or personal experimentation, individuals can stay ahead of the curve in this ever-evolving landscape. The key lies in being open-minded, adaptable, and committed to lifelong learning.

forty-nine

AI and Leadership

With innovations emerging at an unprecedented pace. One such innovation that has taken the business world by storm is Artificial Intelligence (AI). In this chapter, we will explore how AI can be a powerful tool for leaders, enabling them to propel their goals and foster more accurate and faster value delivery within their teams and organizations.

AI, once a concept confined to science fiction novels and movies, has now become a tangible reality that leaders can leverage to drive success. It offers immense potential for streamlining processes, enhancing decision-making, and gaining valuable insights. As an agile leader, embracing AI can prove to be a game-changer in today's fast-paced business landscape.

To fully appreciate the impact of AI on leadership, let us delve into its various applications. One area where AI excels is data analysis. Traditional methods of manual data processing are time-consuming and prone to human error. With AI-powered algorithms, leaders can analyze vast amounts of data in real-time, extracting meaningful patterns and trends that would otherwise go unnoticed. This invaluable information empowers leaders to make informed decisions swiftly.

Furthermore, AI has proven to be instrumental in automating repetitive tasks that consume valuable time and resources. By delegating mundane tasks to intelligent machines, leaders can free up their own time as well as their team's capacity for more creative endeavors. For instance, routine administrative duties such as scheduling meetings or generating reports can effortlessly be automated using AI tools.

However powerful AI may be on its own merits; it truly shines when combined with human expertise. Agile leaders understand the importance of striking a balance between automation and human involvement. They recognize that while machines excel at processing data and performing repetitive tasks efficiently, they cannot replace the unique cognitive abilities possessed by humans.

One notable application of this synergy between humans and AI is predictive analytics. By harnessing historical data through AI algorithms, leaders can gain valuable insights into future trends and potential outcomes. This enables them to make proactive decisions that anticipate challenges and capitalize on opportunities. Agile leaders leverage predictive analytics as a strategic advantage, guiding their teams toward success.

In addition to data analysis and automation, AI also plays a pivotal role in enhancing communication and collaboration within teams. With the advent of virtual assistants and chatbots powered by AI, leaders can facilitate seamless communication channels that transcend geographic boundaries and time zones. These intelligent chatbots can answer frequently asked questions, guide company policies, or even act as personal productivity coaches for individual team members.

Moreover, AI-powered platforms enable teams to collaborate more efficiently by providing real-time updates, organizing project tasks, and facilitating knowledge sharing. Agile leaders recognize the importance of fostering a collaborative environment where team members can thrive collectively while leveraging the power of AI tools to enhance their productivity.

However, leaders must approach AI implementation with caution. While the benefits are undeniable, there are ethical considerations that must be acknowledged. As stewards of their organizations' values and principles, agile leaders must ensure that the use of AI aligns with ethical guidelines and respects data privacy laws. It is imperative to strike a balance between harnessing the potential of AI and safeguarding individual rights.

AI has emerged as a powerful tool for agile leaders seeking to drive success in today's dynamic business landscape. By leveraging its capabilities in data analysis, automation, predictive analytics, communication enhancement, and collaboration facilitation; leaders can propel their goals forward while fostering more accurate and faster value delivery within their teams and organizations.

However transformative AI may be; agile leaders need to remember that it is merely a tool – one that complements human expertise rather than replaces it entirely. By striking this delicate balance between human ingenuity and technological innovation; agile leaders can harness the full power of AI while ensuring ethical considerations remain at the forefront of their decision-making processes.

As we venture further into the age of AI, leaders must embrace this emerging technology and utilize it to its full potential. By doing so, they can drive their teams and organizations toward success while navigating the ever-evolving landscape of the business world. The future belongs to those who seize the opportunities presented by AI and lead with agility.

fifty

Now and Then: The Future of Agile Leadership

Leaders must stay ahead and adapt to emerging trends. As we peer into the future, one significant development that stands out is the rapid emergence of Artificial Intelligence (AI). In this chapter, we will explore twenty ways in which agile leaders can embrace AI to effectively manage projects and deliver exceptional value to customers and users.

1. Intelligent Project Planning:

AI can assist agile leaders in optimizing project planning by analyzing historical data, identifying patterns, and providing insights to make informed decisions.

2. Predictive Resource Allocation:

By leveraging AI algorithms, agile leaders can predict resource requirements accurately, ensuring optimal allocation for each project phase.

3. Real-time Risk Management:

AI-powered risk management systems analyze multiple data sources in real-time, allowing agile leaders to proactively identify potential risks and take preventive actions promptly.

4. Intelligent Task Assignment:

With AI's help, assigning tasks based on individuals' skill sets and workload capacity becomes more efficient, enhancing team productivity and output quality.

5. Automated Testing:

Agile teams can leverage AI-based testing tools that automate repetitive testing tasks while ensuring higher accuracy and faster feedback loops.

6. Voice-Enabled Virtual Assistants:

Agile leaders can utilize voice-enabled virtual assistants powered by natural language processing capabilities to streamline communication within teams or with stakeholders.

7. Sentiment Analysis for Stakeholder Engagement:

AI algorithms can analyze stakeholder feedback from various sources like social media or surveys, providing valuable insights for improved engagement strategies.

8. Intelligent Data Analytics:

Agile leaders can harness the power of AI-driven analytics tools to gain deeper insights from vast amounts of project-related data generated during sprints or iterations.

9. Smart Decision Support Systems:

By integrating decision support systems driven by machine learning algorithms into their workflow, agile leaders can make data-backed decisions quickly and confidently.

10. Automated Documentation Generation:

AI-powered tools can automatically generate project documentation, reducing the administrative burden on agile teams and enhancing knowledge sharing.

11. AI-Powered Continuous Integration and Deployment:

Agile leaders can leverage AI to automate the integration and deployment processes, enabling faster delivery of features while maintaining code quality.

12. Intelligent Sprint Planning:

AI algorithms can analyze historical data, team capacity, and stakeholder priorities to recommend optimal sprint plans for agile leaders, ensuring efficient utilization of resources.

13. Automated Agile Coaching:

Agile leaders can use AI-enabled coaching platforms that provide personalized guidance based on individual team members' needs, fostering continuous improvement.

14. Smart Performance Monitoring:

By utilizing AI-driven monitoring tools, agile leaders can gain real-time insights into team performance metrics like velocity or cycle time, enabling timely intervention if needed.

15. Natural Language Processing for Requirement Gathering:

Agile leaders can leverage NLP capabilities to extract requirements from unstructured data sources like user feedback or support tickets effectively.

16. Intelligent Estimation Techniques:

AI algorithms can analyze past project data to provide accurate estimations for future projects, aiding agile leaders in setting realistic expectations with stakeholders.

17. Smart Prioritization Assistance:

By analyzing various factors such as user feedback, market trends, and business goals using AI algorithms, agile leaders can make informed decisions when prioritizing features or backlog items.

18. Augmented Reality for Collaboration:

Agile teams can utilize AR technologies to collaborate remotely on complex tasks or conduct virtual meetings with stakeholders in an immersive environment.

19. Machine Learning-Driven Quality Control:

By leveraging ML techniques, agile teams can identify patterns in defect data to predict potential quality issues early on and take proactive measures to prevent them.

20. Intelligent Customer Insights Gathering:

Using AI-powered analytics tools that process customer behavior data across multiple channels helps agile leaders gain valuable insights into customer preferences and expectations which inform product decisions.

As an agile leader embracing the future of technology-driven practices is vital for success. By harnessing the power of AI, agile leaders can optimize processes, enhance collaboration, and deliver exceptional value to customers and users. Embracing these twenty ways to incorporate AI into their leadership approach will enable them to navigate the evolving landscape of agile practices with confidence and achieve greater success in their projects.

About the Author

Daniel Silverman is a respected thought leader and agile coach with two decades of Project Management and Agile Leadership experience. He has helped numerous organizations across diverse industries achieve extraordinary results through the power of agile principles. Silverman's unique insights and practical approach make him the ideal guide for your organization's agile journey.

Read more at https://www.linkedin.com/in/danielmsilverman/.